THE
WAMPANOAG

INDIANS OF NORTH AMERICA

THE
WAMPANOAG

Laurie Weinstein-Farson
University of Rhode Island

Frank W. Porter III
General Editor

CHELSEA HOUSE PUBLISHERS
New York   Philadelphia

On the cover   Wampanoag wood splint baskets

Chelsea House Publishers
Editor-in-Chief   Nancy Toff
Executive Editor   Remmel T. Nunn
Managing Editor   Karyn Gullen Browne
Copy Chief   Juliann Barbato
Picture Editor   Adrian G. Allen
Art Director   Giannella Garrett
Manufacturing Manager   Gerald Levine

Indians of North America
Senior Editor   Marjorie P. K. Weiser

Staff for **THE WAMPANOAG**
Associate Editor   Andrea E. Reynolds
Copy Editor   Terrance Dolan
Deputy Copy Chief   Ellen Scordato
Editorial Assistant   Tara P. Deal
Senior Designer   Laurie Jewell
Picture Researcher   Toby Greenberg
Production Coordinator   Joseph Romano

3   5   7   9   8   6   4   2

Library of Congress Cataloging in Publication Data

Weinstein-Farson, Laurie.
The Wampanoag.

(Indians of North America)
Bibliography: p.
Includes index.
Summary: Examines the history, changing fortunes, and
current situation of the Wampanoag Indians.
1. Wampanoag Indians—Social life and customs—Juvenile
literature. 2. Wampanoag Indians—History—Juvenile
literature. 3. Wampanoag Indians—Ethnic identity—Juvenile
literature. 4. Indians of North America—New England—Social
life and customs—Juvenile literature. 5. Indians of North
America—New England—History—Juvenile literature.
6. Indians of North America—New England—Ethnic
identity—Juvenile literature. [1. Wampanoag Indians.
2. Indians of North America—New England]
I. Title.   II. Series: Indians of North America (Chelsea House
Publishers)
E99.W2W45   1988   974'.00497   88-2828

ISBN 1-55546-733-4
    0-7910-0368-X (pbk.)

CONTENTS

INDIANS OF NORTH AMERICA

CHELSEA HOUSE PUBLISHERS

INDIANS OF NORTH AMERICA: CONFLICT AND SURVIVAL

Frank W. Porter III

*The Indians survived our
open intention of wiping them
out, and since the tide turned
they have even weathered
our good intentions toward them,
which can be much more deadly.*

John Steinbeck
America and Americans

When Europeans first reached the North American continent, they found hundreds of tribes occupying a vast and rich country. The newcomers quickly recognized the wealth of natural resources. They were not, however, so quick or willing to recognize the spiritual, cultural, and intellectual riches of the people they called Indians.

The Indians of North America examines the problems that develop when people with different cultures come together. For American Indians, the consequences of their interaction with non-Indian people have been both productive and tragic. The Europeans believed they had "discovered" a "New World," but their religious bigotry, cultural bias, and materialistic world view kept them from appreciating and understanding the people who lived in it. All too often they attempted to change the way of life of the indigenous people. The Spanish conquistadores wanted the Indians as a source of labor. The Christian missionaries, many of whom were English, viewed them as potential converts. French traders and trappers used the Indians as a means to obtain pelts. As Francis Parkman, the 19th-century historian, stated, "Spanish civilization crushed the Indian; English civilization scorned and neglected him; French civilization embraced and cherished him."

Nearly 500 years later, many people think of American Indians as curious vestiges of a distant past, waging a futile war to survive in a Space Age society. Even today, our understanding of the history and culture of American Indians is too often derived from unsympathetic, culturally biased, and inaccurate reports. The American Indian, described and portrayed in thousands of movies, television programs, books, articles, and government studies, has either been raised to the status of the "noble savage" or disparaged as the "wild Indian" who resisted the westward expansion of the American frontier.

7

Where in this popular view are the real Indians, the human beings and communities whose ancestors can be traced back to ice-age hunters? Where are the creative and indomitable people whose sophisticated technologies used the natural resources to ensure their survival, whose military skill might even have prevented European settlement of North America if not for devastating epidemics and the disruption of the ecology? Where are the men and women who are today diligently struggling to assert their legal rights and express once again the value of their heritage?

The various Indian tribes of North America, like people everywhere, have a history that includes population expansion, adaptation to a range of regional environments, trade across wide networks, internal strife, and warfare. This was the reality. Europeans justified their conquests, however, by creating a mythical image of the New World and its native people. In this myth, the New World was a virgin land, waiting for the Europeans. The arrival of Christopher Columbus ended a timeless primitiveness for the original inhabitants.

Also part of this myth was the debate over the origins of the American Indians. Fantastic and diverse answers were proposed by the early explorers, missionaries, and settlers. Some thought that the Indians were descended from the Ten Lost Tribes of Israel, others that they were descended from inhabitants of the lost continent of Atlantis. One writer suggested that the Indians had reached North America in another Noah's ark.

A later myth, perpetrated by many historians, focused on the relentless persecution during the past five centuries until only a scattering of these "primitive" people remained to be herded onto reservations. This view fails to chronicle the overt and covert ways in which the Indians successfully coped with the intruders.

All of these myths presented one-sided interpretations that ignored the complexity of European and American events and policies. All left serious questions unanswered. What were the origins of the American Indians? Where did they come from? How and when did they get to the New World? What was their life—their culture—really like?

In the late 1800s, anthropologists and archaeologists in the Smithsonian Institution's newly created Bureau of American Ethnology in Washington, D. C., began to study scientifically the history and culture of the Indians of North America. They were motivated by an honest belief that the Indians were on the verge of extinction and that along with them would vanish their languages, religious beliefs, technology, myths, and legends. These men and women went out to visit, study, and record data from as many Indian communities as possible before this information was forever lost.

By this time there was a new myth in the national consciousness. American Indians existed as figures in the American past. They had performed a historical mission. They had challenged white settlers who trekked across the continent. Once conquered, however, they were supposed to accept graciously the way of life of their conquerors.

The reality again was different. American Indians resisted both actively and passively. They refused to lose their unique identity, to be assimilated into white society. Many whites viewed the Indians not only as members of a conquered nation but also as "inferior" and "unequal." The rights of the Indians could be expanded, contracted, or modified as the conquerors saw fit. In every generation, white society asked itself what to do with the American Indians. Their answers have resulted in the twists and turns of federal Indian policy.

There were two general approaches. One way was to raise the Indians to a "higher level" by "civilizing" them. Zealous missionaries considered it their Christian duty to elevate the Indian through conversion and scanty education. The other approach was to ignore the Indians until they disappeared under pressure from the ever-expanding white society. The myth of the "vanishing Indian" gave stronger support to the latter option, helping to justify the taking of the Indians' land.

Prior to the end of the 18th century, there was no national policy on Indians simply because the American nation had not yet come into existence. American Indians similarly did not possess a political or social unity with which to confront the various Europeans. They were not homogeneous. Rather, they were loosely formed bands and tribes, speaking nearly 300 languages and thousands of dialects. The collective identity felt by Indians today is a result of their common experiences of defeat and/or mistreatment at the hands of whites.

During the colonial period, the British crown did not have a coordinated policy toward the Indians of North America. Specific tribes (most notably the Iroquois and the Cherokee) became military and political pawns used by both the crown and the individual colonies. The success of the American Revolution brought no immediate change. When the United States acquired new territory from France and Mexico in the early 19th century, the federal government wanted to open this land to settlement by homesteaders. But the Indian tribes that lived on this land had signed treaties with European governments assuring their title to the land. Now the United States assumed legal responsibility for honoring these treaties.

At first, President Thomas Jefferson believed that the Louisiana Purchase contained sufficient land for both the Indians and the white population.

Within a generation, though, it became clear that the Indians would not be allowed to remain. In the 1830s the federal government began to coerce the eastern tribes to sign treaties agreeing to relinquish their ancestral land and move west of the Mississippi River. Whenever these negotiations failed, President Andrew Jackson used the military to remove the Indians. The southeastern tribes, promised food and transportation during their removal to the West, were instead forced to walk the "Trail of Tears." More than 4,000 men, women, and children died during this forced march. The "removal policy" was successful in opening the land to homesteaders, but it created enormous hardships for the Indians.

By 1871 most of the tribes in the United States had signed treaties ceding most or all of their ancestral land in exchange for reservations and welfare. The treaty terms were intended to bind both parties for all time. But in the General Allotment Act of 1887, the federal government changed its policy again. Now the goal was to make tribal members into individual landowners and farmers, encouraging their absorption into white society. This policy was advantageous to whites who were eager to acquire Indian land, but it proved disastrous for the Indians. One hundred thirty-eight million acres of reservation land were subdivided into tracts of 160, 80, or as little as 40 acres, and allotted to tribe members on an individual basis. Land owned in this way was said to have "trust status" and could not be sold. But the surplus land—all Indian land not allotted to individuals— was opened (for sale) to white settlers. Ultimately, more than 90 million acres of land were taken from the Indians by legal and illegal means.

The resulting loss of land was a catastrophe for the Indians. It was necessary to make it illegal for Indians to sell their land to non-Indians. The Indian Reorganization Act of 1934 officially ended the allotment period. Tribes that voted to accept the provisions of this act were reorganized, and an effort was made to purchase land within preexisting reservations to restore an adequate land base.

Ten years later, in 1944, federal Indian policy again shifted. Now the federal government wanted to get out of the "Indian business." In 1953 an act of Congress named specific tribes whose trust status was to be ended "at the earliest possible time." This new law enabled the United States to end unilaterally, whether the Indians wished it or not, the special status that protected the land in Indian tribal reservations. In the 1950s federal Indian policy was to transfer federal responsibility and jurisdiction to state governments, encourage the physical relocation of Indian peoples from reservations to urban areas, and hasten the termination, or extinction, of tribes.

10

Between 1954 and 1962 Congress passed specific laws authorizing the termination of more than 100 tribal groups. The stated purpose of the termination policy was to ensure the full and complete integration of Indians into American society. However, there is a less benign way to interpret this legislation. Even as termination was being discussed in Congress, 133 separate bills were introduced to permit the transfer of trust land ownership from Indians to non-Indians.

With the Johnson administration in the 1960s the federal government began to reject termination. In the 1970s yet another Indian policy emerged. Known as "self-determination," it favored keeping the protective role of the federal government while increasing tribal participation in, and control of, important areas of local government. In 1983 President Reagan, in a policy statement on Indian affairs, restated the unique "government to government" relationship of the United States with the Indians. However, federal programs since then have moved toward transferring Indian affairs to individual states, which have long desired to gain control of Indian land and resources.

As long as American Indians retain power, land, and resources that are coveted by the states and the federal government, there will continue to be a "clash of cultures," and the issues will be contested in the courts, Congress, the White House, and even in the international human rights community. To give all Americans a greater comprehension of the issues and conflicts involving American Indians today is a major goal of this series. These issues are not easily understood, nor can these conflicts be readily resolved. The study of North American Indian history and culture is a necessary and important step toward that comprehension. All Americans must learn the history of the relations between the Indians and the federal government, recognize the unique legal status of the Indians, and understand the heritage and cultures of the Indians of North America.

Archaic Period projectile points and scraper

EARLY
INDIAN
LIFE

It was the Wampanoag Indians who shared their thanksgiving harvests with the Pilgrims in the 1620s. It was the Wampanoag who gave the Pilgrims Indian corn, squash, and beans, thereby insuring the survival of the first permanent European settlement in New England, the Colony of New Plymouth. The Wampanoag taught the Pilgrims about the lay of the land that the colonists named New England and about how to protect themselves from the harsh winters.

The history of the Wampanoag Indians began long before the 17th century and long before any European set foot on the North American continent. Twelve thousand years ago, the earliest inhabitants of northeastern North America were leaving their indelible mark on the land, a mark that archaeologists are still uncovering today.

At various sites, archaeologists have found arrow- and spearheads, pieces of pottery, bones, and evidence of fires in the form of burnt soil. By studying these sites and artifacts, they have been able to learn about how the people of North America lived in the thousands of years before Europeans arrived. Because there is little left from this time, archaeologists have to work with the sparse evidence they find. One of the first things they do is attempt to determine the age of a site and its artifacts. Study of the artifacts found in northeastern North America has led archaeologists to identify three distinctive prehistoric periods of human civilization: Paleo-Indian, Archaic, and Woodland. (See chart on page 14.)

Although we do not have very much information about them, we do know that Paleo-Indians (*Paleo* means old or ancient) inhabited New England some 12,000 to 10,000 years B.P. (before the present). From the artifacts that remain, we know that they used fire to cook their food and manufactured stone tools for use as hunting weapons and to prepare foods, skins, and other materials. Archaeologists uncovered hearths with burned bone (evidence that the Indians cooked game for food)

Approximate Date	Cultural Period	Key Events
25,000–12,000 B.P.*	Paleo-Indian Period	Ancestors of Indians arrive in North America, probably via a land bridge over the Bering Strait
12,000–10,000 B.P.		Foraging and big-game hunting
10,000–3,000 B.P.	Archaic Period	Hunting, gathering, and fishing
3,000 B.P.–16th century	Woodland Period	Development of horticulture, pottery, and bow and arrow
16th–18th century	Contact Period	Indians meet and trade with Europeans; diseases infect Indians

*Before the present

and stone tools at Bull Brook, near Ipswich, Massachusetts, and at Wapanucket, near Middleboro, Massachusetts, two areas where Paleo-Indians camped.

Paleo-Indians are often referred to as big-game hunters because some of the animals they hunted were huge. One important game animal was the now-extinct mastodon. The Indians also hunted small game such as caribou, musk ox, and giant beaver. Their survival was largely dependent upon the hunting ability of the men. If a man did not bring home meat, a family would have only the wild plant foods that the women gathered, or fish. The Paleo-Indians are referred to as foragers or hunter-gatherers, because their food supply depended on collecting plants, fishing, and hunting.

Paleo-Indians made all their own equipment. Their most important technology was the manufacture of stone tools. These stone tools were used for everything from hunting to making clothing. The Paleo-Indians were quite competent with stone. Some of the tools they crafted are described as fluted projectile points by archaeologists. Projectile points were attached to wooden poles or shafts to become the tips of spears and lances. The term "fluted" refers to channels carved into both sides of the stone points. The end of the wooden shaft fitted into the fluted channel so the point could be firmly attached. These weapons were used to throw at game from short distances. Besides the projectile points, the Indians also made stone knives, scrapers, drills, and awls (tools for piercing holes). These tools were used for cleaning and scraping animal hides, sewing hides into clothing, butchering meat, and woodworking, among other things.

The Paleo-Indians lived in North America toward the end of the Ice Age. Glaciers had covered most of the continent, but they were slowly melting. As the glaciers retreated northward, the sea level rose. The weather was cold and severe. In about 15,000 B.P., the northeastern glacier stretched from Long Island to Nova Scotia. Then the climate warmed and the ice began to melt. By 13,000 B.P. the glaciers had retreated, and the eastern coastline of North America had about the same contours as it has today. The receding glaciers deposited rocks, and melting glacial ice created many of the region's bogs and swamps. (In New England the results of the Ice Age are still visible today.) The warmer climate allowed new plants and trees to grow.

As their environment changed, the early Indians made changes in their way of living. A new style of life developed. This marked the beginning of a new period, the Archaic Period, which lasted from 10,000 B.P., the end of the Ice Age, to 3,000 B.P. Archaic Indians enjoyed a favorable environment that was no longer as cold and dry as it had been during the Paleo-Indian Period.

The big game did not survive the change to a warmer, milder climate. However, small animals such as deer, as well as a wide variety of fish, plants,

The Paleo-Indians, who depended on hunting for much of their food, were big-game hunters. When the men killed a mastodon, it provided food for their families for many weeks.

and trees, were well suited to the new climate. The Indians had a wealth of new resources. In order to work with these resources, the Archaic Indians manufactured many types of stone tools and projectile points. Just as the Paleo-Indians can be identified by their projectile points, so, too, can the Archaic Indians be identified by the variety and types of stone points that they manufactured.

Archaic Indians developed numerous types of projectile points. Archaeologists have identified many of their styles and named them. Usually the names refer to the places where the points have been found. *Squibnocket* points are small, triangular in shape, and made of white quartz. *Merrimack* points are usually long and thin and have stemlike ends. These styles can be identified not only by their shape, material, and location but also by the time when they appear in the archaeological record. The Squibnocket points were made by Indians living sometime between 6,000 B.P. and 3,700 B.P. Merrimack points are associated with Indians living at an earlier time—between 8,000 B.P. and 6,000 B.P.

The more technologically advanced Indians of the Archaic Period developed many more types of stone tools than the Paleo-Indians. As people became more skilled in working stone, they learned to create tools suited to specific tasks. Some tools were used for hunting game, others for butchering and cutting meat. Still others were used for chopping wood, shaping other stone tools, drilling shells, scraping hides, and building canoes to navigate nearby rivers and streams. This variety of tools made them better able to use the food materials and other resources of their environment. This in turn made it possible for a large population to live in a community. The differing tool types of the Archaic and Paleo-Indian periods may also reflect the differing identities of the people living at those times, the same way that clothing, language, or food vary among ethnic groups today.

In southeastern New England, archaeologists have uncovered many sites from the Archaic Period. Titicut and Seaver Farm, both near Taunton, Massachusetts, and Wapanucket, near Middleboro, Massachusetts, are the

A harpoon of the early Archaic Period, found at the Wapanucket site near Middleboro, Massachusetts, consists of a stone projectile point lashed onto the end of a wooden shaft.

names of just a few of the important sites. Of these, the Wapanucket site offers the most material for study. Archaeologists have found evidence there of three little round houses. Each house had a circular framework with a doorway formed by two overlapping walls. Archaeologists speculate that each house was occupied by a single family.

We know that the Wapanucket Indians buried their dead with care because archaeologists have uncovered burial grounds. From the remains at these sites, they know that the Indians first cremated the dead and then buried the ashes and bones in a huge pit. Personal artifacts of the deceased were carefully placed alongside them, perhaps for the dead to use in their next life.

A combination of fear and reverence for nature figured into the beliefs and practices that the prehistoric Indians developed. They depended on the natural environment to meet all their needs and had to recognize their powerlessness against the forces of nature that resulted in droughts, storms, and floods. The Indians recognized their own mortality.

The Woodland Period, between 3,000 B.P. and 1,500 B.P., saw new technology enter the Indians' way of life. Influenced by peoples in the southwestern and southeastern areas of North America, they learned how to craft pottery, use a bow and arrow, and cultivate the land.

Until the invention of pottery, Indians relied on baskets, wooden bowls,

Soapstone (steatite) pots and dishes from the Archaic Period. Before they learned how to make pottery, the Indians used steatite as containers for food. When wet, steatite was easy to shape with harder stone tools.

and steatite (a soft and easily carved stone) vessels to hold their food. Women probably wove the baskets and carved the steatite vessels. Men carved wooden bowls. These containers were not efficient for cooking food; basketry and wood are flammable and steatite is too heavy to carry about. Fired clay pottery, however, was perfect for both cooking and storing food.

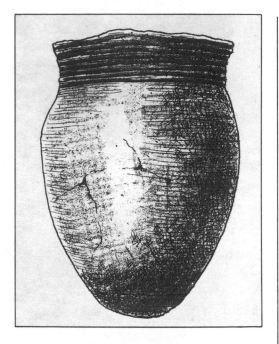

An example of the type of pottery container that Woodland Period Indian women made for storing and cooking food.

The Indian women were the potters. To make pots and other vessels, they first collected clay from riverbanks. They then broke the clay up into fine particles with their hands, wet it, and kneaded it. To prevent the pots from cracking while being fired, the women added either crushed shell or stone to the clay. Native-American pottery of the Woodland Period was typically shaped like a cone and sometimes had a rim at the top. The pots stood upright when their pointed bottoms were placed into soft earth or sand.

The development of the bow and arrow was important for the Woodland-Period Indians. These Indians still man-ufactured projectile points, but they also began to make smaller, specialized points called arrowheads, which they attached to the end of a narrow, straight wooden shaft. As a weapon, the bow and arrow was more accurate and powerful than the thrown or thrust spear. Hunters could attack their prey from a greater distance, which afforded them a margin of safety that the spear did not provide. Archaeologists have recorded a wide variety of arrow- and spearhead styles from this prehistoric period.

Horticulture provided an important supplement to the Indians' diet. Cultivating crops provided the Indians with a more reliable food supply than did hunting, gathering, or fishing. Once they started planting, the Indians also began to settle into villages for a few months out of the year so the women and children could look after the crops. The new foods could be stored after they were harvested. The people no longer had to be constantly on the move in search of the game, nuts, or berries that they had depended on to survive.

The introduction of horticulture and the creation and use of pottery and the bow and arrow thus made possible a generous supply of food. This allowed Indian communities to grow in size. During the Woodland Period, the Indian tribes of southern New England were established. A tribe consisted of one or more communities sharing a common territory, language, and culture. Among them were the Wampanoag, Narragansett, Niantic, Pequot-Mohegan, Nipmuck, and Mas-

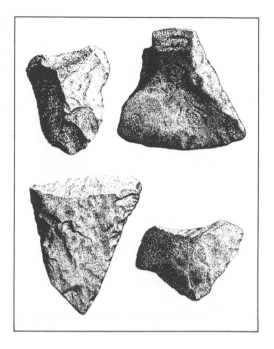

Woodland Period stone tools that were probably used as hoes. One is lashed to a wooden handle. They were used for weeding fields and breaking the soil.

Agricultural tools of the Woodland Period found in Rhode Island, Massachusetts, and Connecticut.

sachusett tribes. All of these Indians lived in farming villages near the coast during the spring and summer months. They farmed and fished and stored food for the winter. In fall and winter, the Indians left their villages and moved farther inland. Here they hunted and fished along rivers and other waterways.

Archaeologists have identified various sites where tribes lived in the Woodland Period. Some of the better known sites are the Locust Spring site in Greenwich, Rhode Island; Potter Pond in Warwick, Rhode Island; and Titicut and Wapanucket in southeast-

ern Massachusetts. The last two sites were repeatedly occupied by prehistoric Indians for thousands of years, from Paleo-Indian times into the Woodland Period. Consequently, artifacts from the Paleo-Indian, Archaic, and Woodland Periods are represented at these sites.

Archaeologists and historians cannot be certain that any one of these sites was definitely occupied by the Wampanoag. They do know, however, that some were occupied, if not by direct ancestors of the Wampanoag people, then by people who shared a similar cultural heritage.

(continued on page 22)

THE FIRST THANKSGIVING

Every year, on the last Thursday of November, families in the United States join to celebrate Thanksgiving with a feast. This holiday is said to date back to November 1621, when the Pilgrims at Plymouth Colony shared a meal with the local Indians, the Wampanoag, and gave thanks for their first harvest in New England.

Since the 17th century, artists have portrayed their visions of the first Thanksgiving. Many works show a romanticized view of the event and have helped to perpetuate a particular image of the Pilgrims and Indians and their harvest feast: dark-clothed, somber English men, women, and children, seated at a long table next to their feather-bedecked Indian neighbors, eating squash, pumpkins, cranberries, and, of course, turkey.

In fact, we know little about the actual event that was the source of our Thanksgiving holiday. The only contemporary references to the event are from Governor William Bradford and Edward Winslow, Pilgrims who participated in the thanksgiving feast. No accounts from the Wampanoag exist.

L. G. Ferris, The First Thanksgiving, *c. late 19th-early 20th century.*

Jennie Brownescombe, The First Thanksgiving at Plymouth, *1914*.

Bradford, who evidently proclaimed the celebration, does not specifically mention the feast in *Of Plimoth Plantation*, his history of Plymouth Colony. Of the Pilgrims' first harvest and their food he wrote: "They began now to gather in the small harvest they had, and to fit their house and dwelling against winter, being all well recovered in health and strength and had all things in good plenty. . . . Besides waterfowl there was great store of wild turkeys, of which they took many, besides venison, etc. Besides they had about a peck [or eight quarts] meal a week to a person, or now since harvest, Indian corn to that proportion."

In a December 11, 1621, letter to a friend in England, Winslow more specifically described the thanksgiving feast:

> Our harvest being gotten in, our governor sent four men on fowling, that so we might after a special manner rejoice together after we had gathered the fruit of our labors. . . . We exercised our arms, many of the Indians coming amongst us, and among the rest their greatest king Massasoit, with some ninety men, whom for three days we entertained and feasted, and they went out and killed five deer, which they brought to the plantation and bestowed on our governor.

The actual date of the first Thanksgiving is unknown, but to 20th-century Americans this does not seem to matter. The holiday, with its familiar traditions and images of Pilgrims and Indians, has become a celebration for all Americans to share, whatever their origin.

(continued from page 19)

The Wampanoag were known to their neighbors as the *Pokanoket*, which means "place of the clear land." However, Adrian Block of Holland, who traveled to the Narragansett Bay area in the early 17th century, referred to the Indians he encountered there as the "Wampanoo." Later, English travelers to the area called them the Pokanoket. Eventually the name Wampanoo developed into Wampanoag and, in the 17th century, this name and Pokanoket were both used to refer to the same group of Indians. After the middle of the 17th century, "Wampanoag" had for the most part replaced "Pokanoket" as the Indians' name. *Wampanoag* means "People of the East" or "People of the Dawn."

At the beginning of the 17th century, between 21,000 and 24,000 Wampanoag inhabited the southeastern portion of present-day Massachusetts, the islands off of its shores, and the eastern part of Rhode Island. Their territory contained forests of oak, maple, and pine, as well as rivers, streams, and wetlands. When the Pilgrims met them in 1620, the Wampanoag were competent farmers, fishers, hunters, and gatherers. All of these occupations provided them with a generous supply and variety of foods. The Wampanoag had an established system of government and religion. The family was at the heart of their society. Children learned from their parents about their future adult roles.

Mortars (left and right) and pestles from the late Woodland Period used for grinding corn.

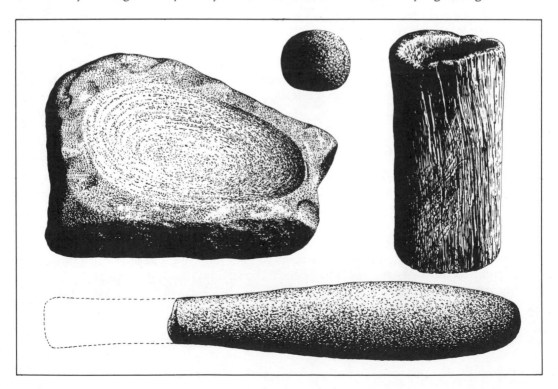

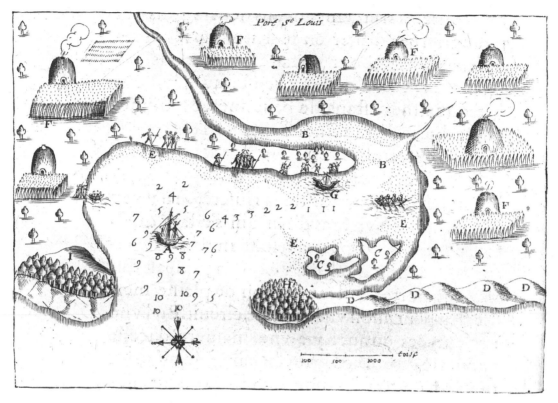

A 1605 map drawn by the French explorer Samuel de Champluin. The place he named Port St. Louis was later called Plymouth by the English. The map shows Indian fields and houses located near the shores of what is now Cape Cod Bay.

With the arrival of the Pilgrims and other foreigners from Europe, the Wampanoag's territory was infringed upon and their style of life disrupted. The Europeans would introduce new technologies and diseases and would even change the Indians' relationship to the land. The European presence was never far off. It continued to press and pull, and before the end of the 17th century it had destroyed the traditional way of life of the Wampanoag. The Wampanoag people's relationship with non-Indians has shaped their history from 1620 to today.

In the 18th and 19th centuries, as the newcomers prospered and took over the land, the Indians struggled against poverty and discrimination. In spite of the hardships, most of the geographically scattered Wampanoag communities survived. Their communities have grown in both size and strength during the 20th century. Today, the Wampanoag attempt to keep their Indian traditions as well as to learn and benefit from the ways of their non-Indian neighbors. ▲

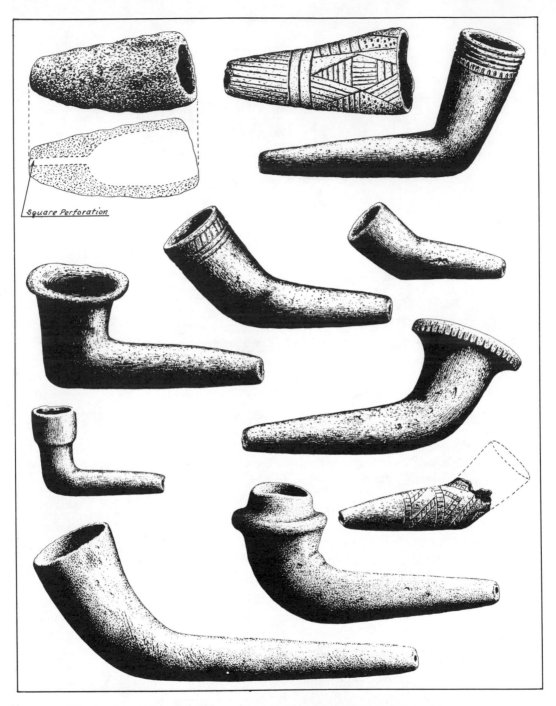

Pipe bowls made of clay, from the Woodland Period, found in Massachusetts, Rhode Island, and Connecticut.

Square Perforation

GETTING FOOD
IN THE
17TH CENTURY

The first account by Europeans of the Wampanoag may have been written in 1524. Giovanni da Verrazano mentions meeting two Indian "kings" when he was exploring the coasts of present-day Rhode Island and Massachusetts. However, the most informative written records of the Wampanoag come from the 17th century, the major period of their first contact with Europeans. The newcomers encountered Indians as they explored and established colonies in New England. Travelers and colonists wrote about the New World and its inhabitants for eager English friends and readers. The records of this period—diaries, court records, books, and letters—are a rich source of information about the Wampanoag. The Indians' own accounts of their history and way of life were passed down orally from generation to generation.

In May and June 1602, Bartholomew Gosnold explored what is now Cape Cod and its offshore islands. A member of his crew, John Brereton, described meetings with local Indians in his journal. On May 15, Brereton, Captain Gosnold, and three others went ashore to explore a large shoal that they had named Cape Cod. Brereton later wrote, "We espied an Indian, a yong man, of proper stature, and of pleasing countenance; and after some familiaritie with him, we left him at the sea side and returned to our ship." About a week later, Gosnold discovered the islands south of Cape Cod and named one of them Martha's Vineyard and another, Elizabeth's Island. Of the inhabitants of these islands, Brereton wrote, "We saw manie Indians, which are tall big boned men. . . . They gave us of their fish readie boiled, whereof we did eat and judged them to be fresh water fish: they gave us also of their Tabacco, which they drinke [smoke] greene, but dried into powder, very strong and pleasant." After exploring the coasts of present-day Massachusetts and Rhode Island, Gosnold and his crew returned to England.

The first manuscript page from Governor William Bradford's Of Plimoth Plantation, *a history of the Pilgrim settlement that also gives information about the Wampanoag.*

Two of the most important colonial records of the Indians are William Bradford's *Of Plimoth Plantation* and Edward Winslow's *Good News from New England.* Bradford was the first governor of Plymouth Colony and Winslow was the colony's governor in 1633, 1636, and 1644. Their histories concern the daily life of the colonists, their system of government, and the colony's relationship to the Indians. John Winthrop, Jr., who helped found Ipswich, Massachusetts, wrote about the Indians in journals and letters as well. The court records from Plymouth Colony also contain useful information about the Wampanoag. These documents describe hearings on land disputes and treaty signings. Another major source of information about New England Indians in general is *A Key into the Language of America* by Roger Williams, a pastor in Plymouth and, later, founder of Providence, the first non-Indian settlement in Rhode Island. In this book Williams describes the Narragansett Indians, a group that was culturally similar to the Wampanoag.

All these written records provide a detailed account of the Wampanoag's food-getting practices. They were primarily farmers, but their food also came from hunting, fishing, and the gathering of fruits, seeds, and roots of wild plants. Their survival depended on carrying out these activities according to a seasonal schedule. The Wampanoag cleared and planted their fields in spring. Spring and summer were also the best seasons for digging clams and catching herring and other fish. Crops were harvested in early fall. Fall and winter were the best seasons for hunting deer and bear.

Farming is a relatively recent activity in the Northeast. Some of the first evidence of farming in this general area

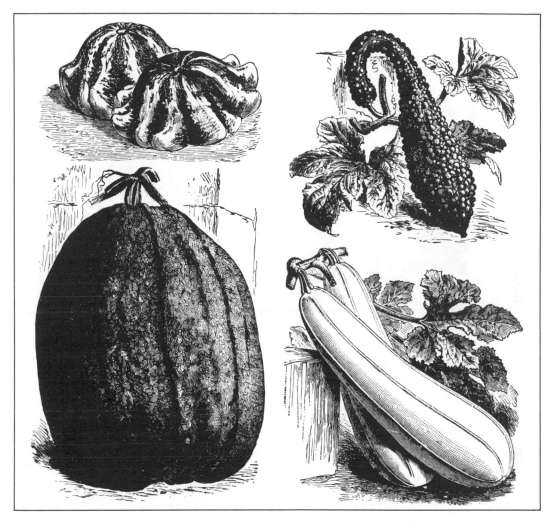

Gourds, white squashes, and pumpkins were some of the crops grown by the Indians.

dates back to A.D. 1060. At the Round Top village site in present-day New York State, archaeologists have found evidence of seeds and horticultural tools. Farming brought many changes to Indian society. The food they were able to produce and store could feed a larger population; communities grew, and people had time to do more than just find the next meal.

The Wampanoag grew a few staple crops for food: corn, beans, and squashes. The Indian corn plant was of the Northern Flint variety. Each plant bore only two small, relatively short ears of dark-colored corn. Wampanoag

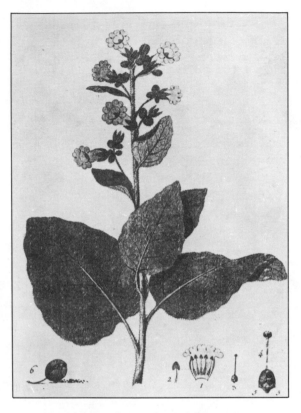

The Indian tobacco plant, in a 1786 illustration

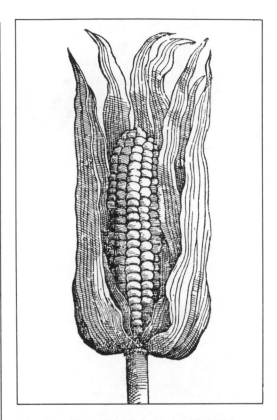

The first illustration of corn published in Europe, which probably dates from 1535. Corn was a major food of the Indians.

squashes included the pumpkin, bush scallop, white bush scallop, zucchini, summer crook neck, and acorn varieties. The beans were a type of pole bean, whose stems must cling to a support. The beans were planted so that they climbed the cornstalks as they grew.

The Wampanoag also raised gourds and tobacco. Gourds, when dried, provided hollow containers that could be used to hold water and food. Tobacco, smoked in pipes passed from one per-

son to another, served as a way of extending hospitality and friendship to visitors. Many colonists were offered a tobacco pipe by their Indian hosts.

All of these crops required the Wampanoag's constant attention during the growing season. If they did not tend their fields, other plants would spread and choke the crops. Animals such as crows and mice would devour seeds and young crops. The Wampanoag therefore labored to clear, plant, weed, and watch over their fields.

In the spring, after the danger of the last frost had passed, the Wampanoag began to prepare their fields. The men and women cleared the fields and the women usually planted the seeds. All crops were planted together in the same plot. They planted the corn in "corn hills," spaced three feet apart. Three or four kernels of corn were buried together. The Indians used large seashells as scoops to move the soil. Alongside the corn they planted beans so that the growing bean plants would interlace with the corn as they both matured. Squash seeds were planted in the areas between the corn and bean hills.

When the corn was as high as the length of a hand it was time to weed. A second weeding might be necessary when the stalk "beginith to grow high," according to John Winthrop. The Wampanoag had several types of tools for farming: hoes, spades (flattish stones used for root digging), and stone dibbles (digging sticks) or "corn planters" (used to make holes for seeds). Roger Williams described three kinds of hoes used by the Indians: a hoe for general use, a weeding hoe of either quahog (clam) shell or deer scapula (shoulder bone), and a "breaking-up" hoe made of stone that was triangular in shape

Separating dried kernels from an ear of corn, in a 20th-century demonstration.

and probably used to help tear out the stumps of trees that had been felled to clear fields.

The first harvest took place about four months after the planting. The young, green corn and the first squashes and beans were then ready to eat. At this time the Wampanoag held a green corn ceremony to thank the Creator for the first fruits of the season.

Some of the young ears of corn were roasted and eaten, but most of the corn was threshed as it was gathered to separate the kernels from the husk, and then the kernels were dried in the sun. The drying was done on mats woven of grass or reeds. When dry, the kernels were stored in pits dug in the earth. Winthrop described the pits as "barnes well lined with withered grass and with matts and then covered over with the like and over that with earth." If the Wampanoag did not store sufficient quantities of corn to last the winter, they had to rely upon gathered plant foods, such as acorns and other seeds, to tide them over until spring.

Hunting, fishing, and foraging supplemented the Wampanoag diet. The hunting season began almost as soon as the harvest was over. The men hunted large game such as deer, bear, and occasionally moose (southeastern New England was at the southernmost

A bowl made of elm burl (extra woody growth), from the mid-17th century. It is believed to have belonged to the sachem Metacomet (King Philip).

Hunting deer with a hedge drive. Several Indian men drove deer into a long wedge formed by hedges or fences, while other hunters waited to shoot the deer.

extent of moose territory, so they were not common). The men also caught small game such as beaver, raccoon, rabbit, and muskrat.

In the hunting season, everyone traveled inland to hunting lodges often located in valleys. These lodges, known as *weetos*, or wigwams, were semipermanent structures. In the spring, when the Wampanoag returned to their farming communities, they would take the mats and bark coverings that served as walls for the lodges and leave behind the structural pole frames. Roger Williams described this move by the Narragansett Indians:

Ten or twentie [go] together, and sometimes more, and withall (if it be not too farre) wives and children also, where they build up little hunting houses of Barks and Rushes . . . and so each man takes his bounds of two,

three, or foure miles, where hee sets thirty, forty or fiftie Traps, and baits his Traps with that food the Deere loves, and once in two dayes he walks his round to view his Traps.

Colonist Thomas Morton wrote about how deer were hunted:

Trappes made of their naturall Hempe [rope made out of plant fiber], which they place in the earth; where they fell a tree for the browse [for the animals to nibble its leaves], and when hee [that is, the deer] rounds the tree for the browse, if hee tread on the trapp, hee is horsed up by the legg, by meanes of a pole that starts up and catcheth him.

Another method of trapping used by the Wampanoag was the hedge drive. Some Wampanoag would chase the deer into a narrow passageway be-

Several methods of fishing, drawn in the 16th century by English colonist John White.

tween hedges and trees. Other hunters waited at the end of this gauntlet to spear the deer who were hemmed in.

Fishing was second in importance to agriculture as a source of food for the Wampanoag. Although spring and summer were the best times for fishing, fish could be taken year round from both rivers and oceans. Shellfish of many kinds were available all year, too: oysters, scallops, soft-shell crabs, quahogs (hard-shell clams), and large sea clams. Lobsters were not eaten but used as bait for more favored types of fish.

The Wampanoag took freshwater fish from New England's many lakes, ponds, and rivers. Some ocean fish, such as alewife, herring, and bluefish, migrated inland to these freshwater sources to reproduce and could be taken there.

The Wampanoag caught fish with spears, lines of twisted plant fiber attached to bone hooks, nets made of plant fibers, and weirs, fencelike structures of long wooden stakes built across a river or stream. Large fish were killed with spears. A Wampanoag would quietly wait in his canoe until he spotted his prey. Then he would quickly throw his spear into the water, hoping to hit the fish. The spear was attached by a line to the canoe so that if a speared fish swam and struggled to free itself, it would drag the canoe and fisher along with it. Nets were usually strung across the mouth of a river or cove in the spring to trap spawning fish as they swam upstream.

A productive location for a weir would be used generation after generation. One of the best known fish weirs from this period was in the area of what is now downtown Boston. Now called the Boylston Street Fish Weir, it was discovered at the turn of the century when contractors began to expand downtown Boston and were excavating the foundation of a new building. Archaeologists have determined that it was first built in 4,500 B.P. It consisted of thousands of wooden stakes placed side by side across the bay and driven into the muddy bay floor. At high tide, water rose above the weir and fish swam into the huge, two-acre trap.

When the tide receded, they were retained behind the stakes and could easily be taken by the Indians as needed. Unfortunately, the site has been destroyed by repeated leveling of office buildings and excavation for new buildings.

Foraging by the women and children provided food all year. In the late spring and throughout the summer, a variety of berries—strawberries, raspberries, huckleberries, and currants—were ripe and ready to eat. The Wampanoag also gathered wild leeks and onions during this time. The roots of the groundnut were dug in late summer. The fruits and seeds were also eaten. Acorns and chestnuts were gathered in the fall, and the long, edible tuber of the Jerusalem artichoke was dug in late fall and throughout the winter.

Farming, hunting, fishing, and foraging were essential to the day-to-day, year-to-year survival of the Wampanoag. To organize their activities and ensure that the bounty of nature continued to be available to them, the Indians relied on political and spiritual practices. These customs both protected and directed their food-getting activities. ▲

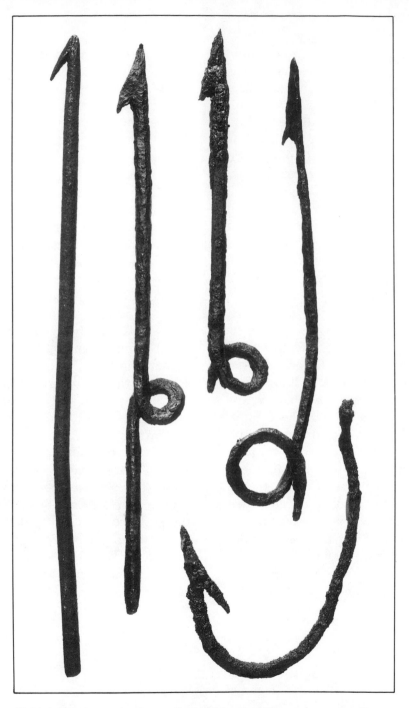

Fishhook and spearheads, probably from the 17th century, found on Martha's Vineyard.

LEADERSHIP, FAMILY,
AND
RELIGION

When the Pilgrims first came upon the Wampanoag, their leader was Massasoit. He was known as the supreme sachem (leader), and he governed with a group of lesser sachems. It was Massasoit who signed the first treaty with the Plymouth Pilgrims in 1621. In this treaty, the Wampanoag pledged to neither hurt the Pilgrims nor steal from them, and the Pilgrims agreed to support the Wampanoag in any confrontations with other Indians in the area.

Massasoit's domain included villages governed by seven lesser sachems. Each village was a contained community, its adults organized to provide food and other essentials for residents of all ages. Over the course of a year villages changed in size as people moved in or out to carry on their food-getting activities.

The village functioned also as a social and political unit under the leadership of a sachem. Sachemships were passed from father to son, or sometimes to a daughter, if there were no male heirs. However, most of the sachems were male. Once sachems inherited their post, they had to prove themselves worthy of the position by demonstrating good judgment and knowledge.

The New England sachems were not authoritarian rulers. Their influence and power were very much subject to the extent of popular support they enjoyed. According to Daniel Gookin, a 17th-century colonist, if sachems did not fulfill their duties, the people "should desert them, and thereby their strength, power, and tribute would be diminished."

Sachems were responsible for the people's welfare. To keep their people healthy and comfortable, sachems used their expertise to mediate relationships between them and the gods and spirits of the natural world. When these relationships were in harmony, the spirits would provide ample food and shelter for the people and all would be well and prosperous.

Sachems settled disputes among individuals and families and represented the Wampanoag in all dealings with outsiders. Their duties also included granting land to individuals for farming. They then supervised both the planting and harvesting. Roger Williams noted that the sachem also "takes care for the Widow and fatherless; also for such as are aged and in any way maimed if their friends be dead or unable to provide for them."

Sachems did not work alone. Williams describes councils of "esteemed men" who assisted them. Each of these advisers was a *pniese*, or man of great courage and wisdom. A pniese was also a war leader and acted as the sachems' personal bodyguards whenever they traveled outside of a village.

The people thanked sachems for their help. Once a year each community gave their sachem tribute in the form of gifts of food. Some of this food was often given to widows, orphans, or older members of the tribe. Two 17th-century reports by Edward Winslow and colonist Matthew Mayhew concern this tribute. Winslow wrote that the people are asked to "bestow much corn on the sachem; they appoint a certain time and place, near the sachem's house, where are brought many baskets of corn." Mayhew writes that sachems also received "wrecks of the sea, skins of beasts killed in their dominions, and many like things."

The sachems ruled, but it was the families that kept Wampanoag society functioning. All knowledge was con-

Roger Williams, who came to New England in 1630, wrote extensively about the Indians living in the area of present-day Rhode Island.

veyed from one generation to another through the family. All work that had to be done was carried out by family members. The family unit grew and shrank with the change of the seasons as the work to be done changed. During the fall and winter months, when the Indians were living in their hunting lodges and the men were hunting, the number of people in each family swelled in number.

These large winter families included several generations—grandparents, parents, and children, as well as some relatives by marriage. Aunts, uncles, and friends could be included in this family unit, too. In the fall there was plenty of work for all members, and in the winter food was shared. All lived together in one large weeto made of wooden poles covered with woven grass mats or bark. As many as 50 individuals might live in these structures.

In 1674, Daniel Gookin observed that the Indians' houses were of several sizes according to their activity and ability; some twenty, some forty feet long, and broad. Some I have seen of sixty or hundred feet long. . . . In the greater houses they make two, three, or four fires at a distance one from another.

During the spring and summer months, the size of the family unit or household decreased. The summer

(continued on page 42)

A weeto, or wigwam, under construction in a 20th-century recreation at Plimoth Plantation in Plymouth, Massachusetts. The mats for the interior of the house are woven of bulrush and those for the outer walls of cattail stems. The museum includes a reconstructed 17th-century Indian village.

Glass sack (wine) bottle

A 17TH-CENTURY
INDIAN CEMETERY

Like other Indian tribes of New England, the Wampanoag interred their dead in designated burial grounds. Some of these Indian cemeteries have been discovered and archaeologists have excavated them in order to learn more about the culture of the early inhabitants of New England.

An important 17th-century Wampanoag burial site was identified in Warren, Rhode Island, in 1913. The Burr's Hill cemetery was near Sowams, the principal village of Grand Sachem Massasoit, and Mount Hope, the village of Massasoit's son, Metacomet (King Philip), after he became sachem. In the spring and summer of 1913, archaeologists uncovered 42 graves at Burr's Hill and studied the remains. Most of the individuals were found lying on their sides, with their knees drawn up toward the chest. This type of burial has been seen at many other sites.

Also in the graves were a variety of objects. There were pestles, hoes, axes, and other tools, as well as broken pieces of pottery. The Burr's Hill site is significant because an abundance of European-manufactured goods was also found in the Indian graves. Iron and copper kettles, glass bottles, china plates, and pewter- and silver-plated iron spoons were among the items recovered.

The many kettles and spoons had been acquired through trade with Europeans. Because of the strategic location of Burr's Hill, the Indians met many Europeans eager to trade for the Indians' furs. The existence of European goods in graves shows that the Indians quickly learned to use and value these technologically advanced items.

Archaeologists and anthropologists do not know exactly why the Indians buried household objects with their dead. It is apparent that these items were valuable to them. Some indicated the deceased person's role in life. For example, hoes and pestles were buried with women because they cultivated the land and prepared food. Some early settlers wrote that the Indians believed certain items would be needed in the afterlife. Whatever the reasons are for burying objects with the deceased, the items themselves, at such sites as Burr's Hill, have helped us understand the life of the 17th-century Indians.

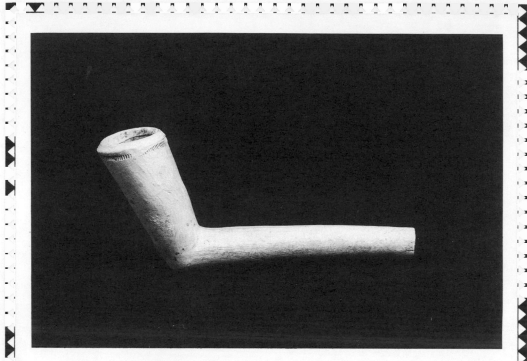

Clay pipe made for trade

Gin bottle

Earthenware jug

China plate with blue heraldic design

(continued from page 37)

family consisted of just a few family members. The weetos were smaller and were not permanent. In the farming season, the Indians spread out to work the land, reestablished their farming villages, and worked in smaller units.

Men and women each had specific roles and tasks in Wampanoag society. Fathers taught their sons how to hunt and trap game. Boys also learned from their fathers how to manufacture flint tools such as arrowheads, stone scrapers, and knives. Mothers taught their daughters how to farm, gather and prepare foods, make clothing, and weave the mats that were used to construct the weeto.

The 17th-century colonists observed the work of the Indians. They saw the men making tools, which was sedentary work, and they knew that they hunted game. They also saw the women working in the fields, preparing foods, and weaving. Many colonists misunderstood the Indians' division of labor. They thought the Indian males

In a 20th-century demonstration at Plimoth Plantation, a Wampanoag woman weaves a cattail mat for the outer wall of a weeto.

were lazy, and that the women did all the work. Edward Winslow of Plymouth Colony wrote that the

> women live a most slavish life: they carry all their burdens, set and dress the corn, gather it in, and seek out for much of their food, beat and make ready the corn to eat and have all household care lying upon them.

The colonists judged the Indians' tasks by their own European-based standards. For instance, they were accustomed to the women working inside the house, and they considered hunting a sport. The colonists did not understand that Indian men and women both worked for the mutual benefit of their society. Furthermore, the women were not "slaves" but could leave their husbands if they were mistreated. Usually a Wampanoag woman would return to the family of her parents if she left her husband.

When a boy was about 11 years old his skills and resourcefulness were tested. The Wampanoag initiation, marking the child's entry into adulthood, was described by Isaack de Rasieres, who visited Plymouth in 1620 from the Netherlands:

> When there is a youth who begins to approach manhood he is taken by his father, uncle, or nearest friend, and is conducted blindfolded into the wilderness. [After several months alone, the young man returns home where,] if he is fat and sleek, a wife is given to him.

Edward Winslow, who came to New England on the Mayflower *in 1620, served three terms as governor of Plymouth Colony and wrote* Good News from New England.

When a boy had proved himself, the Indians usually celebrated with a feast and dancing.

An important concept in Indian society was reciprocity, or mutual exchange between two individuals. Reciprocity was especially apparent in the Wampanoag's hospitality toward others and in their spiritual beliefs.

Travelers who were away from home, Indians and non-Indians alike, could count on the hospitality of the

Massasoit and other Wampanoag meeting with English leaders from Plymouth to sign a treaty of friendship in 1621. The Indian Squanto served as interpreter at this meeting. This bas-relief is on the National Monument at Plymouth, Massachusetts.

Wampanoag. Roger Williams described their generosity:

> Whomsoever cometh in when they are eating, they offer them to eat of that which they have, though but little enough prepar'd for themselves. If any provision of fish or flesh come in, they make their neighbours partakers with them.
>
> If any stranger come in, they presently give him to eate of what they have; many a time, and at all times of the night (as I have fallen in travell upon their houses) when nothing hath been ready, have themselves and their wives, risen to prepare me some refreshing.

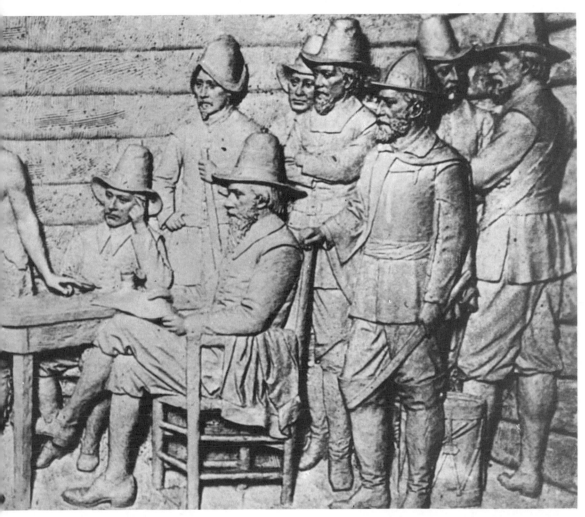

Wampanoag individuals were generous because they knew that they too would be hungry travelers at one time or another. If they offered food and shelter to someone in need, then when their turn came to travel they would be welcome in another's home.

Reciprocity was also at the heart of the Wampanoag's religion, in their sense of having a relationship to all things in the universe. Deer, bear, rocks, trees—everything that existed—had its own special spirit. An Indian out on a hunting trip would appeal to the spirits of the animals to bring him success so that his family would not go hungry. Hunters offered prayers to the animals, and the deer and other animal spirits would reciprocate by allowing themselves to be caught. Hunters were careful not to offend the spirits by killing more animals than they needed.

Whenever the Wampanoag enjoyed a bountiful harvest or a good hunting season, they held a celebration to thank the spirits. Edward Winslow described one such ceremony: "When the Wampanoag would obtain any great matter, [they would] meet together and cry unto him; and so likewise for plenty, victory, etc., sing, dance, feast, give thanks." Sometimes the Indians offered the spirits beads, knives, and other kinds of tools.

The spirits were not the only ones thanked for their generosity. The Creator was thanked, too. The Wampanoag called their Creator *Kiehtan*, and they believed that he held the power of life and death over all the universe. The Indians' most precious food—corn—was a gift from Kiehtan.

The Wampanoag had religious leaders who instilled in them such feelings as humility and thankfulness. Such a person was called a *powwaw*. Roger Williams recognized that the powwaw served functions similar to those of pastors in his own society, but he was puzzled by some of the ways in which the Indians expressed their religious feelings:

These [powwaws] doe begin and order their service, and Invocation of their gods, and all people follow . . . joyne . . . in a laborious bodily service, unto sweatings, especially of the priest [powwaw], who spends himself in strange antick gestures.

Powwaws also conducted special initiation rites for boys and girls who showed promise of special powers. For instance, a future pniese endured vomit initiation rites. The powwaws administered the bark of certain trees to induce vomiting. These rites were intended to test the strength of the initiates and, combined with fasting, induce visions of *Hobbamock*, the devil. The young Indians conversed with Hobbamock and made a covenant of protection with him.

A powwaw served as a religious leader and also as the Wampanoag's physician. One of the powwaw's duties was to supervise the sweat bath. This was a ritual used to either purge the body of disease or to cleanse and refresh it.

The Wampanoag believed that sickness was caused by evil spirits or by Kiehtan's anger. To work cures, the powwaw conducted a ceremony to remove the cause of illness. He would chant, roar, groan, and do everything possible to get rid of an individual's sickness. Colonist William Wood described the theatrical performance of the powwaw:

. . . after violent expressions of many a hideous bellowing and growning, he makes a stop, and then all the auditors with one voice utter a short Canto; which done, the Pow-wow still proceeds in his invocations sometimes roaring like a Beare, other times groaning like a chased boar, smiting on his naked brest and thighs with such violence, as if he were madde. Thus will hee continue sometimes halfe a day, spending his lungs, sweating out his fat, and tormenting his body in this diabolical worship.

This was the world over which the supreme sachem Massasoit presided. For most of the 17th century, the Wampanoag lived peacefully with their new neighbors from England. The Indians helped the newcomers survive in their environment by introducing them to new crops and planting and cooking methods.

In the 17th century, Massasoit's two sons succeeded him as supreme sachem. Wamsutta, or Alexander, as he came to be called, was the eldest and first son to succeed him, in 1661. However, his tenure in office was short-lived; after about a year as sachem he died. Wamsutta was succeeded by Metacomet, or King Philip, in 1662. Both sons strove to maintain a peaceful coexistence with their neighbors. However, conflicts were bound to arise. Two very different ways of life were meeting. Forces far from the lowlands of the Plymouth Colony were about to get involved with the Wampanoag and the Pilgrims. ▲

The death of Indian leader Metacomet, or King Philip, near his head-quarters at Mount Hope 1676. The defeat of the Indians in King Philip's War marked the end of their efforts to halt English settlement in New England.

STRUGGLE
AND
SURVIVAL

King Philip's War of 1675–76 grew out of land conflicts between the New England colonists and the Indians. As more and more settlers arrived, increasing amounts of land were taken for farms and towns. The newcomers encroached on the Indians' seasonal fishing and hunting grounds and sometimes took over cleared farming land. Relations between Indians and colonists became strained as the Indians found settlers living in their traditional fall and winter camping areas. Eventually the settlers of Plymouth Colony made their territorial boundaries the same as those of the Wampanoag.

The Wampanoag began to air their differences with the colonists in the Plymouth Colony courts in the late 1650s. The Indians first became knowledgeable about the English court system when the colonists brought them to court to register land purchases. Court records are filled with accounts of disputes over boundaries, cattle trespasses, and illegal purchases of land.

Boundary disputes and cattle trespass problems were particularly troublesome. The English raised livestock but were careless about fencing their grazing areas. As a result, their cattle roamed onto Indian planting lands, destroying the crops. Some colonists purposely allowed their cattle to roam. They believed that if they continually harassed the Indians, the Indians would move away, which would then open up more land for English settlement.

Sometimes the English resorted to more blatant trickery to obtain Indian land. A few of the court records mention that the Wampanoag were plied with liquor by colonists and then forced to pay for the liquor with land.

All these land conflicts escalated during the 1660s and 1670s. King Philip tried to maintain the treaty of friendship that his father Massasoit had signed with the Pilgrims. Mounting tensions and suspicions on both sides, however, led Indians and colonists to arm for

A steatite tobacco pipe believed to have belonged to King Philip. The pipe was found at Burr's Hill, a 17th-century Indian burial ground in Rhode Island not far from King Philip's headquarters.

war. The Plymouth colonists brought Sachem Philip into court several times and forced him to sign new oaths of fidelity to the colony. Nevertheless, the establishment of new Plymouth settlements on the fringes of the original colonial territory, near Indian villages, severely strained already poor relations.

The spark for war was the murder of an Indian whom King Philip and his followers alleged was a spy for the English. The colonists took three of Philip's men to court for causing the Indian's death and accused Philip of instigating the murder. The Indians were tried under English law, convicted, and hanged. Philip was outraged. Colonists traveling through Wampanoag lands reported that the Indians were armed and ready for war.

King Philip was responsible for confederating Indian tribes throughout New England—such as the Narragansett and Nipmuck—in a war against the colonists. (Some scholars believe that his efforts resulted in the adoption of *Wampanoag* as the name for all of the small groups of Indians in southeastern Massachusetts, Rhode Island, and the off-shore islands.) Banded together, the Indians hoped to put a halt to further English settlement. The Indians' first attack was on a few colonists' homes in Swansea, Massachusetts, in July 1675. The town was on the edge of Plymouth Colony. The Indians continued to raid and burn colonial settlements, particularly other towns on the fringes of colonial territory. The colonists retaliated, raising armies of men to fight the Indians and burning Indian villages, killing hundreds of Indian men, women, and children. Colonists also burned the fields of the Indians' staple food supply—corn.

There was a difference, however, between the Indians' and the colonists' fighting styles. Indian warfare was smaller in scale. Fewer men were killed, and women and children were spared. The large-scale warfare of the Europeans, which involved armies of men and organized marching and firing of rifles, horrified the Indians. In contrast, many of the English were disappointed by the wars against the Indians because Indian warfare sometimes consisted merely of harassing the enemy and not the full-scale battles to which they were accustomed.

Among the Indians, war was usually a family matter, governed partly by their precepts of reciprocity. If a warrior was killed, members of his family might kill the aggressor or a member of the aggressor's family. Indian law gave families the responsibility for avenging any wrong or injury suffered by a family member.

Much of New England's fields and forests were destroyed in King Philip's War. Famine and infighting weakened the Indians. As their strength waned,

Assawompsett Pond in Massachusetts, photographed in 1919 from the location of Metacomet's lookout during King Philip's War.

Metacomet, or King Philip, in an 18th-century engraving by the patriot and silversmith Paul Revere. The print was published by Thomas Church, whose father, Benjamin Church, had fought in King Philip's War.

they began to turn themselves in to the colonists. Many who were captured or became prisoners in this way were either condemned to death or sold as slaves to sugar plantations in the West Indies.

King Philip held out until the bitter end. With a small band of faithful sup-

porters, he retreated to his home at Mount Hope in Bristol, Rhode Island. Colonial militia closed in on them in August 1676. Philip was killed in the chase that ensued, thereby ending King Philip's War.

The Indians were badly defeated. They had been outnumbered, overpowered, and after a year of warfare, they were starving. At the end of the war, the Wampanoag lost their land and their independence. The years following King Philip's War were demoralizing to the surviving Wampanoag Indians. Now the colonists governed the land.

After the war, the New England colonists viewed Indians as either enemies or conquered subjects. They passed laws regulating all Indian affairs. The colonies clearly marked boundaries between their own communities and the Indians' to separate the two groups. If the conquered Indians went outside of the areas where they resided, they had to pay a forfeit of three months of service to "whomsoever shall apprehend and convict them."

The supervision of the Wampanoag Indians was handled by the government of New Plymouth Colony. When Plymouth was absorbed into the Massachusetts Bay Colony—the neighboring colony that had been established by Englishmen in 1630—in 1691, Indian affairs came under its jurisdiction.

Massachusetts Bay Colony continued to regulate Wampanaog affairs until the American Revolution (1775–83). After that war ended, both the state of

Massachusetts and the federal government directed the Indians' affairs.

After King Philip's War, the Wampanoag people had no central location. Most of the Indian villages in Rhode Island and Massachusetts (except for those on Cape Cod) had been devastated by the war. The Indians were now widely scattered in communities throughout Massachusetts and its offshore islands, and Rhode Island. The Wampanoag who had been captured and not shipped to the West Indies were sold into servitude to colonists and worked as indentured servants on the colonists' farms for a period of years.

The Indians were further dislocated because many were assigned to reservations. Even before King Philip's War, the colonial governments had begun sending Indians to reservations. Some of these were farming villages where the Indians were taught agriculture. Others were communities for Indians who had converted to Christianity. These reservations were supervised either by the colonial governments or by church-sponsored missionaries.

Josiah Cotton, grandson of the Puritan clergyman John Cotton, was a missionary among the Wampanoag in the beginning of the 18th century. His diary lists the Indian groups near the town of Plymouth to whom he regularly preached the gospel. Many Indians wanted to hear him speak. When the Indians knew he was visiting a particular family, they would go to that family's house and hear the gospel, too.

The Massachusetts Bay Colony's official seal after 1675. Plymouth Colony became a part of the Massachusetts Bay Colony in 1691. The Indian on the seal is saying "Come over and help us."

Many Wampanoag took English surnames as their own. They would often choose the names of the white families with whom they were friendly.

During the late 17th and early 18th centuries, more Wampanoag were assigned to reservations, and laws were passed to protect the Indians living there. These laws provided for the appointment of guardians or "overseers" of the reservations. The overseers were non-Indian officials charged with representing the Indians in all dealings with the colonists. They also managed the Indians' land, money, and other assets.

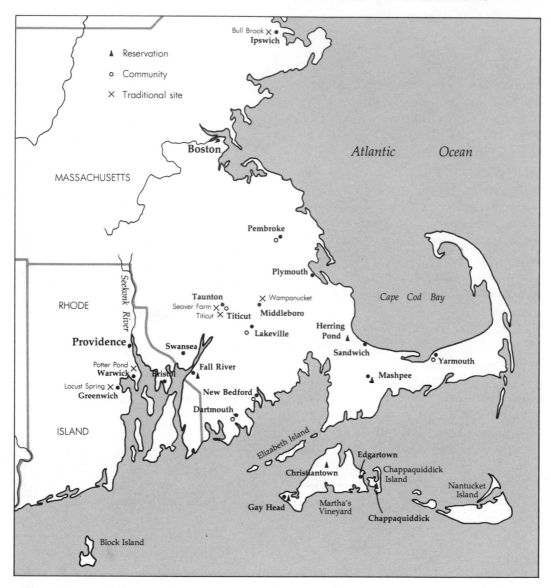

This reservation system did not always serve the Indians' best interests. Many groups suffered extreme poverty and eventually ceased their existence as a unified group. Departure from the reservations due to marriage or by choice also contributed to the disappearance of these Indians.

The Wampanoag living near Fall River, Massachusetts, were granted a permanent reservation in 1707. They built a meetinghouse and school. The community was also served by a white preacher who regularly attended to the group's spiritual needs.

The court records of the colonists describe some of the problems that the reservation Wampanoag had with their colonial neighbors. At Titicut, Massachusetts, for example, the Indians claimed in 1715 that the colonists abused land-use agreements. Indians occasionally leased their own lands to colonists to farm or cut timber. However, the colonists did not always pay the money due to the Indians. Sometimes they even refused to vacate the Indians' land when the period of the lease was over.

The Wampanoag on Cape Cod, Martha's Vineyard, Nantucket, and the other islands off the Massachusetts coast were relatively untouched by King Philip's War. These areas had been on the periphery of the fighting. Daily life continued as usual in their communities. Two Indian centers in this area would grow in size over the years: Gay Head, at the tip of Martha's Vineyard, and Mashpee, near the town of Centerville on Cape Cod.

In the 18th and 19th centuries, three Wampanoag Indian reservations existed on Martha's Vineyard: Chappaquiddick, Christiantown, and Gay Head. Chappaquiddick and Christiantown both suffered from numerous health and land problems. Eventually the Indians there deserted the reservations to find work in neighboring non-Indian communities.

Gay Head remained a strong, vital Indian community. The reservation had been started in 1711, when English missionaries purchased land for the use of Wampanoag living on Martha's Vineyard. One of the most influential and well liked of these missionaries was Thomas Mayhew, Jr. When Mayhew disappeared at sea, the Indians memorialized him by placing stones on the site where he had last preached to them before embarking on his voyage. This stone memorial was named Place on the Wayside, and it can still be seen in present-day Edgartown.

The Gay Head reservation Indians, like all other Wampanoag, were plagued by numerous problems in their efforts to preserve native lands. The Gay Headers repeatedly appealed to the colonial government over land sales and the leasing of lands to the colonists. Land was vital to their identity as Indians not only because they lived from the resources of the land, but also because they saw themselves as caretakers of the land for the Creator. In the 18th and 19th centuries, the Wampanoag used the Gay Head lands in traditional ways. A large tract was set aside for the whole community, and all reservation members could use it as they desired for farming, hunting, or fishing. Smaller tracts of land were owned by individual reservation members and used for house and garden plots. This combination of communal and individual land use was protected by the community's sachem, who rep-

Gay Head, Martha's Vineyard, in spring, in an early 20th-century photograph. The Wampanoag believe that the giant Maushop was responsible for the lay of the land on the island.

resented the Gay Headers in their dealings with non-Indians.

The history of the Wampanoag at Mashpee on Cape Cod is well documented, thanks to the missionary Gideon Hawley, who wrote a full account of his activities with the Indians there. In the early 18th century, Mashpee had been set up as a plantation. Like most colonial New England towns, it had undivided, or common lands that every-

one could use as needed. But whereas other towns also had individually owned house lots and farmlands, Mashpee's land policy was unique. The person who cleared a plot was entitled to use it for as long as he needed it, and he could, in turn, pass on his use rights to his children.

Mashpee did well as an Indian plantation until about 1746, when the Massachusetts Bay Colony stepped in and tried to regulate the Indians' affairs. The colony appointed several overseers, who began to lease Indian land to non-Indians. This created many problems and resulted in the permanent loss of some Indian lands to colonists. The Mashpee Wampanoag protested. They even petitioned the king of England. The Indians regained some of their land. But they were to have many court battles with the colonists and would not always be successful.

The Mashpee Wampanoag had a policy of allowing nonwhite people to live in their community. They felt a kinship to other groups that were similarly discriminated against by the dominant European society. An early Indian petition to the Massachusetts Bay Colony included a clause requesting

> that we may be allowed to vote on and receive any other Indians or mulatoes to share with us in our privileges or properties. But that any English or white man be expressly debarred settling or living [in Mashpee].

Many blacks and Portuguese took advantage of the Indians' offer to reside in Mashpee. Subsequently, many blacks married Indians, which resulted in a mixed population of people that they called mulattoes. Reverend Hawley lamented that by 1788, the "Black Inhabitants upon these lands are about four hundred who are greatly and variously mixed as we have now only twenty and five males and about one

Terwileema (sometimes referred to as Tewileema) in a photograph taken about 1885, when she was reportedly the last female descendant of King Philip. At that time she lived near Plymouth, Massachusetts, with her two sons and operated a poultry farm.

A figurehead of the squaw sachem Awashonks from a whaling vessel built on Cape Cod in 1830. Near the end of King Philip's War, Benjamin Church had convinced Awashonks and the other Sakonnet Indians to fight on the side of the English against King Philip.

hundred and ten females, who are truly originals and not mixed."

The Mashpee Indians faced many problems in their efforts to preserve their community from the outside world. These problems were similar to those of the other Wampanoag communities. They owed debts to the col-onists and disputed land boundaries with them. They quarreled among themselves. They also suffered from discrimination.

The Wampanoag throughout the area supplied the colonial world with a pool of inexpensive labor. However, when they applied for work in the non-Indian world, they were continually faced with discrimination in the form of low wages, poor working conditions, and cruel remarks from employers and co-workers about their Indian identity. The whaling industry especially bene-fited from the labors of the Wampa-noag. Whaling boats visited the coastal Massachusetts towns of Gay Head, Mashpee, and Fall River, and captains persuaded the Indians to work for them. Sometimes the sailors resorted to trickery to get the Wampanoag to sign up: They gave the Indians liquor and then ordered the drunken Indians to work for them to pay off their liquor debts.

In spite of all the problems, the Wampanoag were able to survive, pre-serve their Indian identity, and main-tain many of their traditional arts. At the same time, the Wampanoag were adopting some aspects of the colonists' life-style. They added European hard-ware and furniture to their homes. Then more and more of them gave up their traditional weeto in favor of the European shingled house. In 1767, most Wampanoag still lived in weetos, but only 10 years later most were living in European-styled homes. By the early 19th century, the Indians' weetos had been almost totally replaced by frame houses. But some of the Wampanoag were too poor to build a weeto, let alone a frame house. These Indians lived in huts and hovels.

The Wampanoag also adopted some aspects of the colonists' religion. Missionaries such as Gideon Hawley instructed them in Christianity. However, the Indians retained many of their own customs, and accepted the Christian message selectively. As a result, their practices were somewhat different from those of the colonists. Missionaries often threw up their hands in dismay at the "state of morals and religion." Gideon Hawley wrote:

> Although we have instances of great temperance and industry, I cannot say but that they are too many of them overtaken at times with intoxication. Our females are many of them temperate; but our young women are loose in their morals; and wives have often been found with child when their husbands came from their long voyages.

But Hawley was also impressed with the skill and industriousness of the Mashpee women. He wrote in 1802:

> Our Indian females are many of them good spinsters, combers and weavers. . . . Our females are some of them very good wives and cloth[e] themselves and husbands in every-day-homespun. . . . Many of our squaws make brooms and baskets.

Joseph "Blind Joe" Amos, an active spiritual leader of the Mashpee Wampanoag in the 1850s. This photograph was probably taken about 1890.

Even though they may not have followed Christian teachings to the letter, the church was important to the Wampanoag. It offered a place to come to every week to socialize with family and friends.

In the 19th century, the Wampanoag became more outspoken in complaining about their grievances. They sent petitions to the state government of Massachusetts and demanded to be

Captain Benjamin Church, who fought the Indians in King Philip's War, later helped the Fall River Wampanoag to gain land back from the English settlers.

heard. In 1833, for example, the Mashpee declared that they would both rule themselves and choose their own ministers. This resolution was sent to the governor of Massachusetts. When the state failed to respond to the Indians' demands, the Mashpee took over the meetinghouse, which then served as both church and school. The state finally consented to the Indians' demands the following year.

Aside from the controversial Mashpee, there were also on Cape Cod the Yarmouth Wampanoag, who owned no reservation lands. They mingled with the surrounding non-Indians, married some of them, and lived and worked in their communities. These Wampanoag lived as the non-Indians did and fared better than some of the other groups.

Other groups of Wampanoag lived in scattered communities throughout southeastern Massachusetts and eastern Rhode Island. The Fall River (or Troy) Wampanoag resided on the eastern shore of North Watuppa Pond near Fall River, Massachusetts. Their community numbered 80 individuals living on 190 acres of land. This land had formerly belonged to a man who was convicted in 1693 of "high misdemeanors" and fled to Rhode Island. Captain Benjamin Church, a colonist who had fought the Indians during King Philip's War, presented a petition to the government of the Massachusetts Bay Colony on behalf of this man. The petition proposed that land be conveyed to the colony in lieu of the damages that the convicted man had been ordered to pay. The land was granted to Captain James Church and "certain members of his company of friendly Indians." The ruling stated that these lands could never be taken away from the Indians and were to remain an "Indian Plantation" forever. In the 19th century, the Fall River Indians still had this land. Although they were land rich, they were poor and lived in hovels. They could not even afford to improve their land for farming. Many sought state aid to stay alive.

A small group of Indians lived at Herring Pond, between Plymouth and Sandwich. This community numbered about 50 individuals in the middle of the 19th century. Other Wampanoag resided near Dartmouth, south of New Bedford, Massachusetts. They did not own any reservation lands but worked and lived in the non-Indian world.

The Namatakeeset (or Manattakeesett) Wampanoag originally lived near the Monument Ponds area of Pembroke, near Plymouth. During King Philip's War they had been ordered to go to Clarks Island, in Plymouth Bay, and forced to relinquish their reservation lands. After the war, they were allowed to return to the mainland, but then they dispersed, seeking work wherever they could find it—in Plymouth, Pembroke, and other communities.

Another small Wampanoag community in the 19th century lived in Middleboro. This group of 10 individuals was originally located on Betty's Neck

A wooden ladle from Middleboro, Massachusetts. A small group of Wampanoag lived near Middleboro during the 19th century.

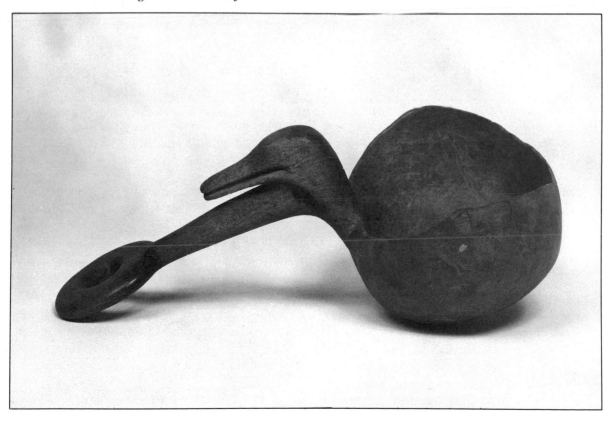

View of New Bedford from the Fort near Fairhaven, *an 1845 lithograph by Fitz Hugh Lane. The Massachusetts port was a major whaling center in the 18th and early 19th centuries.*

in Lakeville, Massachusetts. In the 19th century, some of them became sailors; others moved to New Bedford, Massachusetts.

The Wampanoag of the 18th and 19th centuries lived in separate, scattered communities, but they lived a similar existence. They did whatever work they could find. Some farmed, just as their ancestors had done a hundred years before. These farmers raised the traditional corn, bean, and squash crops. They also grew European grains and potatoes and kept livestock such as horses, cattle, pigs, sheep, and fowl.

The Indians who did not farm, or who farmed very little, either worked as day laborers for non-Indians or went to sea as whalers. The day laborers worked any kind of odd jobs that were available. They hired themselves out as servants, helped construct buildings, mended fences, or tended to farm chores.

The Gay Head Indians maintained

their strong sense of community throughout the 19th and early 20th centuries. They continued to work their land communally for the benefit of the whole tribe. They also supported those in need by leasing land they were not using to non-Indians and sold local clay and cranberries for additional income.

James Freeman, who visited Gay Head in the 19th century, wrote that the "land is broken into hills; and there are no roads. The Indians have twenty-six framed houses and seven wigwams. The framed houses are nothing better than mean huts."

Another visitor, Edward Kendall, described the Gay Head Wampanoag's employment in the whaling industry.

[Whaling] is a favourite employ, to which they give themselves, and to which they are anxiously solicited. Ship-owners come to their cottages, making them offers, and persuading them to accept them; and so rarely is Gay Head visited for any other purpose, that this was supposed, at the light-house, to be my errand. This business of inviting the Indians is a sort of crimping, in which liquor, goods and fair words are plied, till the Indian gets into debt, and gives his consent. . . . The Indians find their fishing-voyages as little for their ultimate benefit . . . and their obstinate addiction to spiritous liquors makes their case still worse: hence, an Indian, that goes to sea, is ruined, and his family is ruined with him.

Four types of harpoons used to hunt whales. Many Wampanoag who lived on Cape Cod and Martha's Vineyard were recruited to work on whaling vessels. Whale oil was used to make candles for lighting.

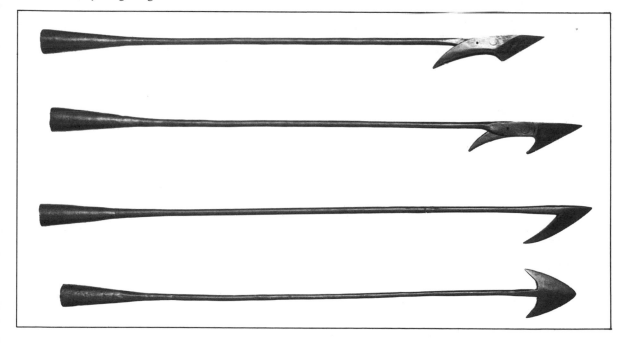

Martha Simon, probably the last Wampanoag living in the Fairhaven, Massachusetts, area, in an 1857 portrait by Albert Bierstadt. Before her death in 1859 or 1860, she was visited by Henry David Thoreau, who wrote in his journal, "She had half an acre of the real tawny Indian face, broad with high cheekbones."

When whaling declined late in the century, Gay Head turned to new economic pursuits, such as construction and tourism, to fill the void.

By the end of the 19th century, the Wampanoag had adopted many European ways. They used European tools for work inside and outside the home. They also wore European clothes and spoke the English language. Despite these changes, the Wampanoag clung to many of their old traditions. One enterprising group of Mashpee Wampanoag went into business, producing baskets, brooms, wooden wares, and other items. They incorporated the Mashpee Manufacturing Company in 1867.

Religion and education were two important matters for the Indians and non-Indians. The state of Massachusetts supported the ministers who settled and preached among the Wampanoag. It also promoted education. Indians on reservations were expected to attend either private or public schools eight months each year. The private schools were located on the Indian reservations and were supported financially by the state. All of these schools taught the English language at the expense of the Indians' native tongue. The schools also encouraged the children to forsake all other aspects of their traditional ways.

If the Wampanoag moved off their state-run reservations or intermarried with non-Indians, they enjoyed the same rights as did other U.S. citizens. But the Indians who stayed on the reservations were always under the supervision of the reservation overseers. These officials managed Indian lands, distributed state money to the tribe, enforced attendance at the schools and churches, and settled any problems between Indians and non-Indians. The

(continued on page 73)

CRAFTS AND THEIR CREATORS

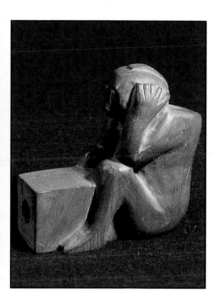

Many Wampanoag today are fusing their Indian heritage with modern artistic tastes to create objects of great beauty. They draw on traditional materials and techniques in their crafts, carving wood and stone, shaping pottery, stringing and weaving beads, and fashioning baskets.

Like Indian people throughout North America, the Wampanoag have always made whatever they needed for practical purposes as well as ornaments for personal adornment. To make this rich variety of objects, they used animal, vegetable, and mineral resources found in their natural environment. Shells, feathers, bones, deer hooves and antlers, bear teeth and claws; tree bark, plant stems, seeds, and roots; stone and clay—these were the raw materials for necklaces, clothing, housing, cooking utensils, cutting tools, and everything else that made existence comfortable.

Working with a variety of materials, the Wampanoag express their creativity, keep their traditions alive, and produce an economic resource for their community. Objects made by Wampanoag artisans are available for sale at Plimoth Plantation in Plymouth, Massachusetts, and The Children's Museum in Boston, as well as at Wampanoag powwows.

Steatite (soapstone) pipe bowl carved by Nanepashemet (Tony Pollard) in 1987, based upon a 17th-century design. Pipe bowls are attached to wooden pipe stems. The Indians traditionally smoked tobacco on important social or formal occasions. The pipe would be passed from one person to another. An offer to a stranger to share the pipe was a sign of friendship.

The colorful cliffs of Martha's Vineyard gave Gay Head its English name. Wampanoag have long used clay from the cliffs to make cooking pots and storage jars, which were fired in kilns to make them strong and watertight. Kiln firing, however, dulled the colors. In the late 19th century, the Wampanoag began to bake their clay pieces in the sun to retain the bright colors. These pots, bowls, and jars were snapped up by visitors to the island. Gay Head pottery is still being produced today.

Necklace of multicolored, sunbaked clay pendants and beads by Gladys Widdis, whose mother and aunt were also potters. In the 1980s, she has expanded the Gay Head pottery tradition to include jewelry.

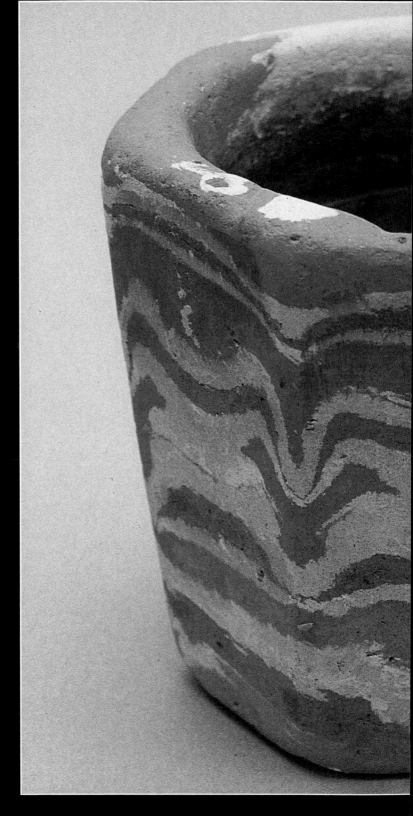

Sunbaked Gay Head pottery, late 19th and early 20th centuries. Celina Manning Vanderhoop created the angular jars by slicing slabs off the sides of hand-modeled pieces. The tall jar, by another member of the Vanderhoop family, was shaped on a pottery wheel.

Although European in origin, glass beads have been an important element in Indian crafts since the 17th century. Today the Wampanoag use beads to decorate traditional buckskin clothing. They also string and weave them to make necklaces, collars, medallions, and other accessories. Right: Collar made by Alice Lopez, using a net stitch and a traditional Plains Indian tubular-beading technique called the gourd or peyote stitch.

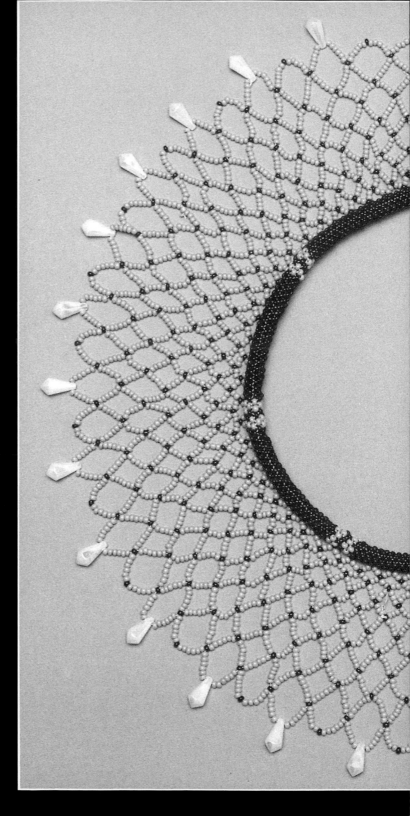

Turtle-medallion necklace by Carol Lopez, mother of Alice Lopez. The turtle is a protective or good luck symbol.

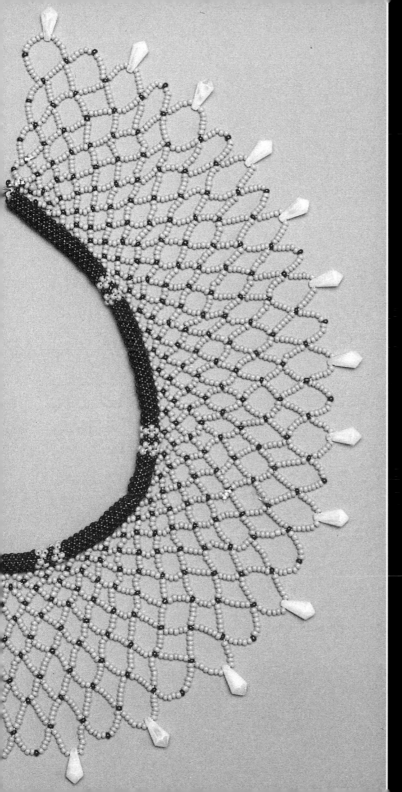

Glass bead and porcupine quill earrings by Linda Jeffers Coombs

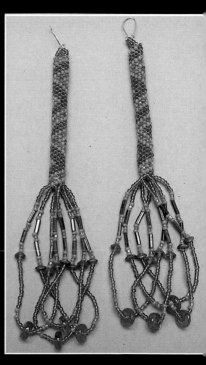

Drop earrings of tubular bead-work by Linda Jeffers Coombs. Two threads cross through each bead to form a woven tube.

Right: *A multicolored bowl by Gladys Widdis. She collects clay at the bottom of the cliffs at Gay Head. Keeping each color separate, she dries the clay and pounds it to powder. When she is ready to make a pot, bowl, or jar, she wets and kneads some clay from each batch. Then she combines the clays to form a multicolored ball. She presses a hole in the center of the ball, expands it, and shapes the vessel with her hands. The piece is then dried in the sun. To sign her work, Widdis draws a wild cranberry, her Indian name.*

Hand-modeled, sunbaked vase made from Gay Head clay by Gladys Widdis.

Leather bracelet with kiln-fired clay disc and seed beads, made in 1976 by Gladys Widdis.

The Wampanoag Indians still produce baskets today, using such traditional techniques as plaiting and plain twining. In twining, two flexible strands (called weavers or wefts) are interlaced around stationary vertical warp fibers. The twined shoulder bag at right, made by Linda Jeffers Coombs, has a finger-woven sash.

Below: *Detail of Coombs' twined bag. It is made of hemp, a plant fiber. The yellow strands were dyed in a bath of boiled onion skins. The other colors were achieved with commercial dyes.*

(continued from page 64)

Wampanoag living on the reservations were not allowed to make their own decisions about how they wanted to live.

During the 19th century, the Gay Head Indians celebrated their identity by hosting powwows (social gatherings that include feasting, dancing, and praying) and pageants. In the pageants, they dramatized the legend of how their mythical hero Maushop brought them to the island. Maushop, a giant who lived on Martha's Vineyard when the first Indians arrived, was responsible for the lay of the land. He had created the colorful cliffs of Gay Head that the Indians later quarried for clay to make pottery. Maushop befriended the Indians and helped them as much as he could until the Europeans arrived. Then he disappeared, leaving only the smoke from his pipe—the coastal fogs—as evidence of his presence.

During the 18th and 19th centuries, some Wampanoag communities disappeared, along with their Indian traditions. However, this was not a continual process; the next century ushered in a renaissance of Indian culture, and the Wampanoag fought for their legal rights as American Indians and U.S. citizens. ▲

A woman wearing a traditional pack basket with a carrying strap, Mashpee, 1914. The baskets were used to gather cranberries and other produce.

THE
WAMPANOAG
TODAY

By the beginning of the 20th century, the Wampanoag people were living much like their non-Indian, working-class neighbors. In the 20th century, their sense of identity as Indians would be revitalized.

During the first few decades of the 20th century, the Pan-Indian movement was sweeping across the continent. This movement, a counteraction to the dominant culture of the United States, was a means for Indians to reinforce their "Indianness." Before the arrival of Europeans, most Indian tribes had kept to themselves, interacting on occasion with similar neighboring tribes to form loose alliances against hostile tribes. Following the contact period, the few confederated activities that had occurred, such as their participation in the French and Indian Wars and King Philip's War, had ended in failure. By the early 20th century, several Indian leaders and tribes had come to see the value in working together to press for their rights against the government bureau-cracy—and to assert their unique Indian identity, which they realized they were losing.

The customs and traditions of the Great Plains Indians came to symbolize the new identity of all Indians. In every section of the United States and Canada, Indians adopted Plains Indian dress along with some of that culture's rich ceremonialism as symbols of Indianness. A key element of the Pan-Indian movement was the powwow, which became an annual event.

Two Mashpee Indians—Eben Queppish and Nelson Simons—brought Pan-Indianism to the Wampanoag. Both of these men had been born on Cape Cod but had moved away from the area. Eben Queppish had spent much of his childhood dressing up as an "Indian" to participate in "Wild West" shows in Montana. He had even appeared in performances with the troop of Buffalo Bill Cody. Nelson Simons had been educated at the Carlisle Indian School in Pennsylvania, a school founded by Richard Henry Pratt in 1879. Backed by the Bureau of Indian Affairs, the school's purpose was to educate young Indians from across the country to be good U.S. citizens. He then returned to Massachusetts to attend law school. During the 1920s, Queppish and Simons joined forces to revitalize the Wampanoag people. They were instrumental in organizing the Wampanoag Nation, a confederacy of communities that would function as a political entity and strengthen its members' Indian identity. In 1928, Indians from Mashpee, Gay Head, and Herring Pond met at Herring Pond to elect leaders for the new nation.

The Wampanoag Nation held its first powwow the following year in

Josephine Wilcox, Bertha Rhodes, and other Mashpee Wampanoag at a social gathering in the early 20th century. Like other Indian tribes across the United States, the Wampanoag adopted the dramatic clothing of the Great Plains Indians, such as buckskin shirts and feathered headdresses, as one way of expressing their Indian identity.

Mrs. Stafford, reportedly a descendant of Sachem Massasoit and Metacomet (King Philip), in a 1923 photograph taken by the anthropologist Frank Speck, who was studying the Indians of the Northeast. At that time she was living in Ipswich, Massachusetts.

George and Daniel Coombs, two young Wampanoag brothers from Mashpee, dressed in their best clothes for this 1901 photograph. By the end of the 19th century, the Indians had adopted the clothing styles being worn by other Americans.

Mashpee and held one annually for many years afterward. The annual powwows lasted several days and gave distant relatives and friends the opportunity to return home for clambakes, dances, and religious services. The Wampanoag donned Plains Indian regalia, including the familiar feathered headdress for the powwow dances.

Holding powwows marked a new beginning for the Wampanoag. Additional dances and ceremonies were added to the Wampanoag's calendar. According to the 1933 New Bedford *Standard Times,* the powwows proved "that the once mighty Wampanoag still live, still follow the customs, the traditions and adhere to the laws and leg-

Eben Queppish, one of the Indians instrumental in organizing the Wampanoag Nation during the 1920s.

ends of their ancestors." Other Massachusetts newspapers, especially from Boston and New Bedford, have reported news of the Wampanoag since the 1930s. They have documented powwows, pageants, tribal political affairs, and noted deaths.

Despite the powwows, for many Wampanoag the first half of the 20th century saw little change from the past.

They continued to live in their communities, work in the outside world, and retain some Indian customs, such as making traditional baskets, preparing salted and smoked herring, and growing Indian corn.

During the 1950s and 1960s, the Mashpee Indians organized classes to teach the traditional ways to their children. The older members of the tribe were worried that the younger people were no longer being taught their Indian heritage by parents and grandparents, so they decided to have the elders who still knew these ways conduct classes. These educational efforts had a significant impact on the sense of identity of the Wampanoag who reached adulthood during the 1970s. The renewal of Indian traditions that began half a century earlier now gained momentum and created a new and outspoken leadership and tribal identity.

Today, the Wampanoag are asserting themselves as Indians. They have a strong voice in both state and federal government affairs. They are pressing for land rights, health and education benefits, and federal recognition. Their sense of pride and unity is a combination of old and new—old traditions are maintained while new ways are adopted.

According to one tribal leader, Red Blanket, the Wampanoag in the 20th century can be characterized as "Indian people working together." The Wampanoag started working together in 1928 to bring about the birth of the

Wampanoag Nation, and they have continued to do so. The governmental system that they established in 1928 is still in place today. It is structured similarly to the 17th-century Indians' system. The Indians are ruled by a grand sachem and a supreme medicine man. These tribal-wide offices are supported by a series of local governments headed by *chiefs*, or leaders, and tribal councils.

In 1975 Ellsworth Oakley, "Drifting Goose," was elected grand sachem of the Wampanoag. Oakley appointed John Peters to the position of supreme medicine man in 1977. According to the Wampanoag, a true medicine man has special powers that enable him to be in contact with the spirits. Peters serves his people in two ways: administering to their spiritual needs, and acting as executive director of the Massachusetts State Commission on Indian Affairs.

A traditional fish trap, Gay Head, Massachusetts, 1931.

Drifting Goose, known as Ellsworth Oakley, grand sachem of the Wampanoag, in March 1987.

In order to revive the Wampanoag, Oakley reorganized the tribe and appointed new leaders in 1975. To explain his actions, he stated at the time that the people had "died out" in some areas or were without leadership and organization. The Wampanoag are now divided into five regional subtribes, each with its own chief. These tribes are the Mashpee (Cape Cod), Gay Head (Martha's Vineyard), Herring Pond (from Wareham to Middleboro), Assonet (from New Bedford to Rehoboth), and Nemasket (the Middleboro region). Oakley appointed new chiefs for all but the Gay Head group. Wampanoag can join any subtribe they chose, but generally enroll in the group nearest to where they live.

The chiefs' duties include calling their people together for meetings and ceremonies and providing leadership and inspiration. The local chiefs also host a variety of activities each year. The Assonets and Nemaskets, for example, host a new year's celebration in May to mark the earth's return to life after the long winter. The Assonets also sponsor a King Philip ceremony to commemorate the renowned Wampanoag sachem, conduct a Green Corn festival in thanksgiving for the harvest, and hold various dinner and dancing socials throughout the year.

The Gay Headers sponsor a number of smaller festivities such as Cranberry Day on the second Tuesday of October. In this ceremony, the Indians offer thanks to the Creator and the cranberry spirits for the first fruits of the cranberry harvest.

The Gay Headers formerly sponsored pageants and powwows. The pageants, including parades with floats, were held at the cliffs at Devils

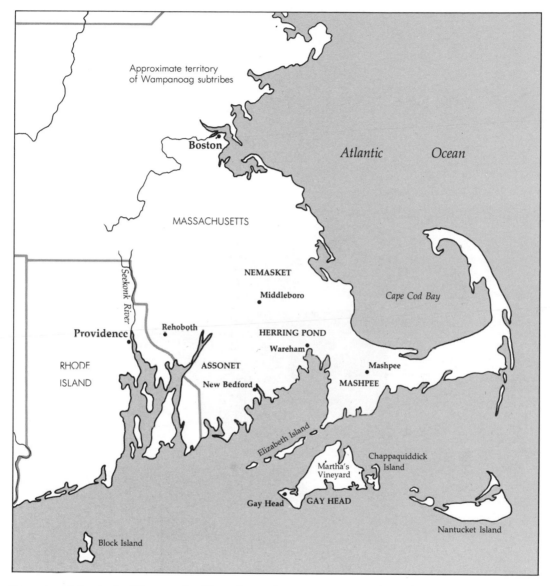

Den on Martha's Vineyard. The Gay Head men carried torches in and lit a huge bonfire. The celebration continued with the telling of the Maushop legend about the creation of Martha's Vineyard. Loss of interest and reduced population led to the end of these pageants and powwows; however, there have been efforts to revive them.

The tribal council of each regional group attends to the group's political concerns and manages the group's

The seashore along Cape Cod, part of the Wampanoag's homeland.

money. Approximately 10 members of the council are elected by consensus. The councils represent the Wampanoag in their dealings with non-Indians. They also maintain the tribal roll and any other records. The tribal roll is the official list of Wampanoag belonging to a particular regional group. It is an important document, not only because it records the Wampanoag's Indian ancestry, but also because it is accepted by the federal government as proof of their Indian identity. Whenever the Wampanoag petition the government or receive any kind of federal or state aid, the tribal roll is relied on to prove who is an Indian and thereby qualified to participate.

The Mashpee and Gay Head tribal councils are the most active. Both of these subtribes' councils have peti-

tioned the U.S. government for federal recognition. When it was denied, these councils contested the decisions. Gay Head won its case in 1987, while Mashpee is appealing the court's 1979 refusal to award recognition.

Recognition by the federal government is based on meeting certain criteria set by the government. Once a tribe is recognized, it is referred to as a "trust-status tribe." Federal recognition is important because it provides the ba-

sis for certain rights and benefits, including education and health services, and financing for building reservation housing and buying new land for future expansion. In 1987, Gay Head received an award of $3 million to provide housing for the elderly and to build a hospital.

As in the past, family and religion are the focal points for the Wampanoag today. Today's Indian family is extended in two ways: One extended fam-

(continued on page 86)

GROWING UP
AS A WAMPANOAG IN
TODAY'S SOCIETY

American Indian history and culture are virtually ignored by the predominantly non-Indian world, despite the fact that the history of the people of North America begins with the Indians. Young Wampanoag today must strike a balance between traditional and modern ways in their lives. Ryan Malonson and Paula Peters are two Wampanoag who have successfully achieved this balance.

Ryan Malonson, from Gay Head on Martha's Vineyard, was born in 1962. Both of his parents, Donald and Pat Malonson, are active in tribal affairs. His father has been chief of the Gay Head Wampanoag since the mid-1950s. His mother serves on the tribal council's board of directors. Ryan's sister, Bettina, works for a business firm in Boston.

Growing up in the Gay Head Indian community helped to cushion Ryan from the prejudices of non-Indian people. As soon as he left for other parts of Martha's Vineyard, however, he heard comments such as, "the Indians will scalp us and take back our land." When he has left Martha's Vineyard he has also occasionally heard negative comments from non-Indians about his heritage.

Ryan is working toward an associate's degree in accounting from Quinabog Valley Community College in Connecticut. He wants to use his training to help the Gay Headers manage their finances.

Ryan learned about his Wampanoag heritage from his family and members of his community. They taught him the legends of his people and about the creation of Martha's Vineyard. He learned about the places that are sacred to the Wampanoag because of their role in the creation of the Vineyard.

One legend concerns the giant Maushop, who, the Wampanoag believe, created the island. In Maushop's farewell to his people he warned of the arrival of non-Indian outsiders. He said: "The White Man will come, you will have to adapt to certain of his ways. But you will always know who you are and what you are."

When Ryan has children he will teach them "to respect life and respect [their] elders." He adds that Indian children must be proud of their heritage and not be ashamed to wear their traditional dress. He would teach his children how to prepare traditional foods and sew their own native dress. He would also teach them the legends of Gay Head and take them to the "old places."

Paula Peters of Mashpee was born in Boston in 1959 to Russell and Shirley Peters. Her parents, who had previously lived in Baltimore and Philadelphia, returned to their native Mashpee to get "closer to their roots." Today both are active in Mashpee affairs. Her father, a past president of the Mashpee Tribal Council, is compiling a photo history of the town of Mashpee. Her mother, who works as a nutritionist at a senior citizens' center, is a member of an Indian education committee that decides how state grants to local schools will be used.

Paula has three brothers: Robert, Russell, and Steven. Robert is a bus driver for the Massachusetts Bay Transit Authority (MBTA) in Boston; Russell is a construction worker in Oakland, California; and Steven is a housepainter in Mashpee. Paula has a seven-year-old son, Steven; she is now divorced. Paula's parents are also divorced. Her father, who no longer lives in Mashpee, and her brothers return home for important tribal and family events. The Peters family is very close, despite both divorces.

Paula is proud to be a Wampanoag Indian. She attributes her pride to two individuals: her mother and Ella Thomas, a Narragansett who has been active in New England Indian affairs. When Paula was a child, her mother sewed a new powwow dress for her every year, making her the envy of all the young Mashpee girls.

Paula met Ella Thomas in 1974, at Plimoth Plantation, a museum in Plymouth, Massachusetts. Paula, as a representative of the Wampanoag, worked with Ella in the museum's Indian program. The program employs Wampanoag to make crafts and build wigwams and canoes in the Indian village at the museum and to lecture to schoolchildren about Indian traditions. Ella transformed Paula from a "beautiful powwow princess into a knowledgeable human being." She instilled in Paula the values of the Indians and taught her about their traditional arts, such as finger weaving and porcupine-quill embroidery. Meeting museum visitors, some of whom had never had contact with Indians, Paula learned to take her identity very seriously.

In 1987 Paula graduated from Bridgewater State College with a degree in business and marketing and now has a position with a Massachusetts company that uses her training. The most valuable lessons Paula feels she can teach her son are to respect life, to be honest with oneself, and to respect all people, regardless of their ethnic background. Paula's lessons to Steven were shaped by her mentors as well as her experiences during the 1960s. As a member of a multiracial community in Boston, she learned to live and share with many kinds of people. The assassinations of John F. Kennedy and Martin Luther King, Jr., the Vietnam War, and the accomplishments of the civil rights movement made her aware of social ills in the United States.

Paula adds that "it is important for us (as Indians) to share what we have with other people, to maintain who we are without losing our identity."

Miniature baskets of rye straw made for sale in 1919. Some straw is dyed green and purple.

(continued from page 83)

ily is the whole community; another is the household group, which usually includes parents, children, grandparents, and anyone else who may need a place to stay temporarily. The household's composition is constantly changing because of this continued hospitality. John Peters notes that ever since he can remember, his family always set five or six extra plates at dinnertime in anticipation of drop-in guests.

The Wampanoag's religion stresses the importance of the Indian community and also encourages individuals to find their own direction and self-expression within the spirit world. Individual expression might take the form of dancing, singing, drumming on traditional drums, or speaking to an assembled group. Wampanoag Indian Nanepashemet, who works at the museum village of Plimoth Plantation, explains that dances and songs are "personal prayers" to the spirit world. The museum, opened to the public in 1949, has employed Wampanoag since the 1960s to participate in public programs to show what life was like in 17th-century Plymouth Colony.

The Wampanoag have three types of religious ceremonies: unity circles, spiritual gatherings, and powwows. The unity circles are the best examples of the way in which the community is maintaining its identity. A unity circle is a gathering of neighbors and family with much singing, drumming, and feasting on traditional foods. Any individual may call a unity circle, and it can be held anywhere in New England, or even throughout the United States. Indians everywhere are invited and a circle may last one or more days.

A unity circle's success depends not on whether many other Indians attend, but on those who do come sharing a "likeness in mind and heart." At the close of the ceremony, the ashes from the ceremonial fire are carefully preserved. They will be carried to the next unity circle where they will be reused. In this way, the Indians' fire can never be extinguished.

Spiritual gatherings can also be held at any time in the year, but they usually coincide with the full moon. There are two major gatherings held either in spring and fall or spring and summer. Some gatherings include the Assonet-Nemasket new year's ceremony and the Assonet's King Philip ceremony.

Of the three types of ceremony, the powwow is the only celebration to which the non-Indian public is invited. The Mashpee powwow, held on the July 4th weekend, is the most important

A Cape Cod Wampanoag fisherman, with his nets.

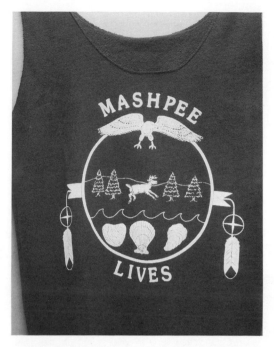 

T-shirts and caps are made by the Wampanoag today. They are for sale at Wampanoag powwows, along with other crafts.

and one of the largest of the Wampanoag powwows. The powwow lasts three days and draws both Indians and tourists from throughout New England as well as other areas. It is one of the most exciting events in the Wampanoag calendar.

It begins with a procession in which the grand sachem and the medicine man lead the tribal officers and dancers into the outdoor arena, where they dance in a circle around the drummers who are waiting there. The drummers sing and pound their drums and the earth pulsates to the beat of their music and the jingle of the bells on the dancers' feet. All performers wear ceremonial garb that is a combination of traditional Wampanoag deerskin clothing and Plains Indian attire. After the opening dances, the grand sachem welcomes the crowd to the powwow. His speech closes with a prayer to both the Creator and the spirits.

Food and craft booths surround the dancers' arena. The food booths offer traditional foods, such as steamed quahogs, clam cakes, and boiled lobsters and corn. The smells of seafood and corn bread cooking over the outdoor fires fill the air. Individuals can purchase the artwork on display, such as jewelry made out of silver and beads, clothing, pottery, and baskets.

All Wampanoag ceremonies emphasize their lifeway, or how one leads one's life. The lifeway is based on traditional values that predate the 17th century, and all that has happened since then. According to Nanepashemet, the Wampanoag respect the "natural order of things." They realize that humans are only one of many types of creatures on earth, and so all living beings must be treated with utmost respect. They also believe that thankfulness must be given to creator spirits for all that exists.

The future of the Wampanoag depends on various factors. For one, it depends on the inspiration of their leaders, and the involvement of the tribal members in choosing their own direction. The Wampanoag must also further strengthen their identity as a unified group, something that they have struggled with in the past, because the tribe has always been made up of scattered groups. Currently, the Wampanoag are drawing on their past heritage to build a new identity in the present. The tribe will also have to face the problems of the lack of federal recognition and economic stability.

But the future of the Wampanoag also depends on the decisions and actions of non-Indians. Tolerance and

A monument marks the spot in present-day Provincetown, Massachusetts, where the Pilgrims first landed on North American soil, on the Wampanoag's homeland.

perhaps legislation are necessary to preserve a cultural heritage dating back thousands of years. We must all share in supporting the heritage of the Wampanoag and other Indians. The diversity of traditions of the peoples of North America enriches us all. ▲

BIBLIOGRAPHY

Bradford, William. *Of Plymouth Plantation, Sixteen Hundred Twenty to Sixteen Hundred Forty-Seven*. Edited by Francis Murphy. New York: Random House, 1981.

Dexter, Lincoln. *Maps of Early Massachusetts: Prehistory Through the 17th Century*. Wilbraham, MA: Lincoln Dexter, 1979.

Gibson, Susan, ed. *Burr's Hill. A 17th Century Wampanoag Burial Ground in Warren, Rhode Island*. The Haffenreffer Museum of Anthropology Studies in Anthropology and Material Culture, vol. 2. Providence: Haffenreffer Museum of Anthropology, Brown University, 1980.

Jennings, Frances. *The Invasion of America: Indians, Colonialism, and the Cant of Conquest*. New York: W. W. Norton, 1975.

Leach, Douglas. *Flintlock and Tomahawk: New England in King Philip's War*. New York: W. W. Norton, 1966.

Lester, Joan. *We're Still Here: Art of Indian New England at the Children's Museum*. Boston: The Children's Museum, 1987.

Marten, Cathy. *The Wampanoag in the 17th Century: An Ethnohistorical Survey*. Occasional papers in Old Colony Studies, no. 2. Plymouth, MA: Plimoth Plantation, 1970.

Peters, Russell. *The Wampanoag of Mashpee*. Somerville, MA: Media Action, 1987.

Russell, Howard. *Indian New England Before the Mayflower*. Hanover, NH: University Press of New England, 1980.

Simmons, William. *Spirit of the New England Indians*. Hanover, NH: University Press of New England, 1986.

Snow, Dean. *The Archaeology of New England*. New York: Academic Press, 1986.

Speck, Frank. *Territorial Subdivisions and Boundaries of the Wampanoag, Massachusett, and Nauset Indians*. Indian Notes and Monographs, Misc. series, no. 44. New York: Museum of the American Indian, Heye Foundation, 1928.

Weinstein-Farson, Laurie. "17th Century Southern New England Indian Agriculture." *Bulletin of the Massachusetts Archaeological Society*, Fall 1986.

Wilbur, Keith. *The New England Indians*. Chester, CT: The Globe Pequot Press, 1978.

Williams, Roger. *A Key into the Language of America*. Edited by John T. Teunissen and Evelyn J. Hinz. Detroit: Wayne State University Press, 1973.

THE WAMPANOAG AT A GLANCE

TRIBE *Wampanoag*

CULTURE AREA *Northeast*

GEOGRAPHY *present-day southeastern Massachusetts and its offshore islands and eastern Rhode Island*

LINGUISTIC FAMILY *Algonquian*

CURRENT POPULATION *1,500 to 2,000*

FIRST CONTACT *possibly Giovanni da Verrazano, Italian, in 1524. (He met with two "kings" who were either Wampanoag or Narragansett.) The first confirmed contact with the Wampanoag was with Bartholomew Gosnold, English, in 1602.*

FEDERAL STATUS *Gay Head Wampanoag recognized, as of 1987; a 1979 ruling against recognition is being appealed by the Mashpee. The other three subtribes of the Wampanoag Nation are unrecognized.*

Algonkian The Indian people living in northeastern United States and east-central Canada whose languages are related and who share numerous cultural characteristics.

archaeology The systematic recovery and study of evidence of human ways of life, and especially that of prehistoric peoples.

Archaic Period The period from about 10,000 to 3,000 years ago, when the way of life of American Indians generally involved hunting and gathering and was characterized by the invention of improved weapons and seasonal migrations for food acquisition.

artifact Any object made by human beings, such as a tool, garment, dwelling, or ornament.

Bureau of Indian Affairs (BIA) A U.S. government agency established in 1824 and assigned to the Department of the Interior in 1849. Originally intended to manage trade and other relations with Indians and especially to supervise tribes on reservations, the BIA is now involved in developing and carrying out programs to encourage Indians to manage their own affairs and to improve their educational opportunities and general social and economic well-being.

Contact Period The 16th through the 18th centuries, when European explorers and traders in North America first met Indians. For the Wampanoag, the time of contact was in the early 17th century or possibly a century earlier.

culture The learned behavior of human beings; nonbiological, socially taught activities; the way of life of a given group of people.

foraging An economic system based on the collection of wild plant foods, animals, and fish; the most ancient human way of obtaining the necessities of life. Foragers are often called hunter-gatherers.

horticulture Production of food using human muscle power and simple hand tools to plant and harvest domesticated crops. Horticulture is commonly women's work. Agriculture, which requires the power of draft animals and larger tools such as plows, is usually men's work.

Ice Age A time in the earth's history when vast ice sheets or glaciers covered much of North America and Eurasia. It ended about 10,000 years ago.

Kiehtan The name given to the Wampanoag's creator; the Wampanoag believed he held the power of life and death.

Maushop A mythical Wampanoag hero who, the Indians believed, created Martha's Vineyard. He befriended the Indians who came to live there.

missionaries Advocates of a particular religion who travel to convert nonbelievers to their faith.

Paleo-Indian Period The period in North America more than 10,000 years ago when the way of life of humans involved hunting large mammals and making specialized stone tools.

Pan-Indian movement An affirmation of renewed interest in Indian identity that spread throughout North America in the early decades of the 20th century.

pnieses Esteemed Wampanoag men who served as advisers and bodyguards to a sachem and also functioned as war leaders.

Pokanoket The name used by neighbors of the Wampanoag and early 17th century English travelers and settlers to refer to these Indians; literal meaning is "place of the clear land."

powwaw A Wampanoag religious leader and curer who supervised rituals and ceremonies.

powwow An Indian social gathering that includes feasting, dancing, rituals, and arts and crafts displays, to which other Indian groups as well as non-Indians are now often invited.

prehistoric Anything that happened before written records existed for a given locality. In North America, anything earlier than the first contact with Europeans is considered to be prehistoric.

projectile points Weapon tips made of stone, attached to wooden shafts to produce spears or lances. The Paleo-Indians produced unique fluted points.

reservation A tract of land set aside by treaty for occupation by and use of Indians. Some reservations were for an entire tribe; others were assigned to more than one tribe.

sachem A Wampanoag leader responsible for the government and welfare of a village.

sweat bath Prolonged exposure to steam for a ritual purpose: to purify an individual, cure disease, or prepare for ceremony and prayer. Usually performed in a sweat house, an airtight hut in which steam is produced by pouring water over heated rocks.

treaty A contract negotiated between representatives of the United States (or European nation) and one or more Indian tribes. Treaties dealt with surrender of political independence, peaceful relations, land sales and payments for them, boundaries, and related matters.

tribe A term used to describe a type of society consisting of a community or group of communities that occupy a common territory and are related by bonds of kinship, language, and shared tradition.

trust-status tribe The name given to a tribe that has been federally recognized. Once a tribe acheives this status, the federal government is responsible for providing it with social, medical, and educational services and protecting the tribe's right to self-government and any trust property.

weeto or *wigwam* A one-room dwelling constructed of a framework of saplings or branches covered with tree bark or woven mats.

weir An enclosure constructed of wooden stakes set into a stream or river for trapping fish.

Woodland Period The period beginning about 3,000 years ago in northeastern North America characterized by the beginning of horticulture, pottery making, use of the bow and arrow, and permanent villages.

INDEX

ACKNOWLEDGMENTS

The author is indebted to many people and institutions for their help in the preparation of this book. The Wampanoag Indians were my greatest source of support and information: Paula Peters, Russell Peters, Ryan Malonson, Donald Malonson, Daisey Moore, Supreme Sachem Drifting Goose, Tribal Medicine Man John Peters, and Chief Alan Maxim of the Herring Pond Wampanoag. Special thanks go to Linda Jeffers Coombs and her family—Joan Patadal, Beatrice Gentry, and Milton Jeffers—and Nanepashemet for help in identifying 19th– and 20th–century photographs.

Anthropologists Dr. Jack Campisi, Dr. Kathleen Bragdon, and Dr. William Simmons referred me to valuable materials on the Wampanoag. The Boston Children's Museum, The Harvard Peabody Museum, The Haffenreffer Museum of Anthropology at Brown University, the Massachusetts Archaeological Society, and Plimoth Plantation allowed me to use their materials. In particular, Joan Lester at the Children's Museum and Marie Pelletier at Plimoth Plantation deserve thanks for their assistance.

Ted Avery, page 65; The Bettmann Archive, pages 20, 21, 26, 27, 28 (*right*), 32, 36, 43, 48, 52, 60, 82–83, 89; Bulletin of the Massachusetts Archaeological Society, pages 12, 16, 17, 18, 19, 22, 24; Hillel Burger/Peabody Museum, Harvard University, cover; Rob Cooper/The Children's Museum, Boston, Mass., pages 66–72, 88, 89; Renée Dekona, pages 80, 87; courtesy Department Library Services, American Museum of Natural History, page 15; FPG International, pages 44–45; Carmelo Guadagno/Museum of the American Indian, Heye Foundation, pages 38, 40, 41, 50, 61; by permission of the Houghton Library, Harvard University, page 23; The Massachusetts Historical Society, pages 30, 53; Millicent Library/Spinner Publications, page 64; Museum of the American Indian, Heye Foundation, pages 34, 76, 77 (*right*); The New York Public Library, page 28 (*left*); Peabody Museum of Natural History, Yale University, page 86; Plimoth Plantation Photo, pages 29, 37, 42, 59; Smithsonian Institution, page 57; Frank G. Speck/Museum of the American Indian, Heye Foundation, pages 51, 56, 74, 77 (*left*), 78, 79; The Whaling Museum, New Bedford, Mass., pages 53, 62, 63; C. Keith Wilbur, *The New England Indians*, 1978, courtesy of the Globe Pequot Press, page 31.

Maps (pages 2, 54, 81) by Gary Tong.

LAURIE WEINSTEIN-FARSON, currently an instructor in sociology and anthropology at the University of Rhode Island and at Mohegan Community College, received her B.A. degree from Colorado College and her M.A. and Ph.D. degrees from Southern Methodist University. An expert in the ethnohistory, material culture, and agricultural systems of North American Indians, she has served as a research associate and guest curator for the Haffenreffer Museum of Anthropology at Brown University and as a visiting scholar at Plimoth Plantation in Plymouth, Massachusetts. Her research and numerous publications have focused on the Native Americans of New England, especially the Abenaki, Narragansett, and Wampanoag.

FRANK W. PORTER III, General Editor of INDIANS OF NORTH AMERICA, is Director of the Chelsea House Foundation for American Indian Studies. He holds a B.A., M.A., and Ph.D. from the University of Maryland. He has done extensive research concerning the Indians of Maryland and Delaware and is the author of numerous articles on their history, archaeology, geography, and ethnography. He was formerly Director of the Maryland Commission on Indian Affairs and American Indian Research and Resource Institute, Gettysburg, Pennsylvania, and he has received grants from the Delaware Humanities Forum, the Maryland Committee for the Humanities, the Ford Foundation, and the National Endowment for the Humanities, among others. Dr. Porter is the author of *The Bureau of Indian Affairs* in the Chelsea House KNOW YOUR GOVERNMENT series.